GILL'S STUDIES IN IRISH LITERATURE
Terence Brown, General Editor

Ironies of *Ulysses*

Other titles in the Gill's Studies in Irish Literature series:

Brian Moore: A Critical Study

John Banville: A Critical Study ⁻

Patrick Kavanagh: Born-Again Romantic

GILL'S STUDIES IN IRISH LITERATURE

Ironies of *Ulysses*

DAVID G. WRIGHT

GILL AND MACMILLAN

Published in Ireland by
Gill and Macmillan Ltd
Goldenbridge
Dublin 8
with associated companies in
Auckland, Delhi, Gaborone, Hamburg, Harare,
Hong Kong, Johannesburg, Kuala Lumpur, Lagos, London,
Manzini, Melbourne, Mexico City, Nairobi,
New York, Singapore, Tokyo
© David G. Wright 1991
Print origination by Irish Typesetters,
Galway
Printed by Billing & Sons Ltd, Worcester

British Library Cataloguing in Publication Data
Wright, David
Ironies of "Ulysses". – (Gill's studies in Irish literature)
I. Title   II. Series
823

ISBN 0 7171–1685–9

To
Claire

Irony. The modern mode: either the devil's mark or the snorkel of sanity.

Julian Barnes, *Flaubert's Parrot*

These days everything is ironic, everything is in quotes.

Time, 3 September 1990

Ironical opposition cheers.

Ulysses

Contents

Preface

Several years ago I submitted to a reputable journal a short article about an instance of irony in the 'Wandering Rocks' episode of Joyce's *Ulysses*. In rejecting this article for publication, the journal remarked that it would be more persuasive if it appeared, not standing alone, but as part of a book-length study of irony in *Ulysses*. The article was subsequently accepted by another reputable journal, but I kept in mind the valuable suggestion—however intended—of a book on the subject. Irony seems essential to *Ulysses*, as to few other texts, and I hoped that a comparative account of the extremely varied ironic modes which Joyce adopts for his novel might be worth writing. Hence, in any case, the present book. In the dedication I acknowledge a recently incurred but keenly felt debt of gratitude.

D.G.W.

List of Abbreviations

Titles of Joyce's works are abbreviated in citations as follows:

CW *The Critical Writings of James Joyce*, ed. Eilsworth Mason and Richard Ellmann, New York: Viking Press, 1959/ London: Faber & Faber, 1959.

D   *Dubliners: Text, Criticism, and Notes*, ed. Robert Scholes and A. Walton Litz, New York: Viking Press, 1969/ London: Jonathan Cape, 1969.

E   *Exiles*, New York: Viking Press, 1973/Harmondsworth: Penguin Books, 1973.

FW *Finnegans Wake*, rev. edn New York: Viking Press, 1958/ London: Faber & Faber, 1958.

L I, II, III *Letters of James Joyce*, Vol. I, ed. Stuart Gilbert, New York: Viking Penguin Inc., 1957, reissued with corrections 1965; Vols II and III, ed. Richard Ellmann, New York: Viking Press, 1966/London: Faber & Faber, 1957, reissued with corrections 1965; Vols II and III, ed. Richard Ellmann, London: Faber & Faber, 1966.

P   *A Portrait of the Artist as a Young Man: Text, Criticism, and Notes*, ed. Chester G. Anderson, New York: Viking Press, 1968/London: Jonathan Cape, 1968.

SH *Stephen Hero*, ed. Theodore Spencer; rev. John J. Slocum and Herbert Cahoon, New York: New Directions, 1963/ London: Jonathan Cape, 1963.

Page references are to the American editions in each case.

Citations from *Ulysses*, ed. Hans Walter Gabler (New York: Garland, 1984), appear without an abbreviated title, and simply specify the episode and line number: (e.g. 14/315). The British edition was published by Bodley Head, 1986.

Full bibliographical details for other books cited appear in the Bibliography.

1

Introduction

Towards the end of James Joyce's *A Portrait of the Artist as a Young Man*, Stephen Dedalus expounds a theory of aesthetics to his friend Lynch. Lynch interrupts Stephen's proclamations with a series of sardonic comments about the real world which might impinge on Stephen's theories, and with specific allusions to his own poverty, an irksome phenomenon which Stephen's aesthetics appear to overlook. Then Stephen's ethereal speech is more radically disrupted by the passing of a noisy cartload of old iron.

That this iron acts as a further, more intensely critical comment on Stephen's speech will be generally accepted, given Joyce's insistently oblique and symbolic manner. Stephen's aesthetics are too rarefied, too remote from the inescapable world of commerce and process, and the load of iron—like Lynch's poverty—embodies the harsh, irreducible physical reality they would seek to ignore. Some readers might say that Joyce's particular choice of old scrap iron (no doubt rusty, and in any case unglamorous and essentially useless) emphasises the implied rebuke to Stephen and denotes the serious limitations in his theory, the large areas of life which he tries to avoid.

A further implication of this scene has been pointed out by Edmund L. Epstein. He observes that Joyce shows the world of physical contingency, embodied in the scrap iron, commenting ironically on Stephen's limitations; thus a sardonic pun appears in the use of 'iron' to convey 'irony'. 'The dray loaded with old iron that interrupts the climax of Stephen's lecture . . . is literally an "ironic" portrait of Stephen's theorizing' (Epstein 115).

Many readers today would accept this further interpretation, which claims that Joyce embodies, in literal form, the name of the figure of speech represented by that very embodiment. We can find a more specific proof of the validity of this reading if we compare the case in the final version of the *Portrait* with an incident occurring in Joyce's earlier version of his autobiographical novel, published post-humously as *Stephen Hero*. There, in a scene which closely parallels the discussion with Lynch in the *Portrait*, especially in its thematic implications, Stephen reads his essay on aesthetics aloud to his mother. Again the world of physical contingency intrudes on Stephen's airy hypotheses; in the *Stephen Hero* incident, that world is embodied in the house-work which Stephen's mother has to undertake as she listens to him. As in the *Portrait*, the ironic implications of the intrusion take physical form as a pun. While she listens to him, Stephen's mother is doing the household's ironing.

Joyce's unconscious was remarkably refined, and this parallel between the two texts is striking and precise. Neither the driver hauling the old iron, nor Stephen's mother doing the ironing, can be even remotely aware of the 'ironic' implications of the act in question, especially of the pun — which in any case exists only in verbal accounts of the incidents, rather than being intrinsic to them.

In *Ulysses* we find a further slight echo of the scene in the *Portrait*. Once again, late in the text, an exposition of Ste-phen's suffers an interruption, and he responds 'Damn that fellow's noise in the street' (15/2119-20). This remark echoes his definition of God, expressed earlier in *Ulysses*, as 'a shout in the street' (2/386), but it also recalls the intrusion of the old iron in the *Portrait*, which operated as a disruptive 'noise in the street' while Stephen was speaking. The link, once noticed, further intensifies the irony operating in the in-stances in both the *Portrait* and *Ulysses*; and such patterns serve in turn to show the subtle effects which irony produces in Joyce's texts.

Irony in literature, most critics would agree, is the use of a 'false' textual surface to direct a reader's attention towards initially concealed premises or implications. The false surface presents a significance which we must reject, or at least modify, but which usually leads us towards a more authentic or appropriate reading by the nature of its relationship to those implications; thus the 'first' meaning, the 'false' one, always contributes a certain amount of semantic input, if only by serving as a flag or a trigger. As Wayne C. Booth says in his discussion of irony, 'the rejected meaning is in some real sense a rival or threat' (Booth 40). Some people assume that the false message must be the 'exact opposite' of the authentic one, in which case the semantic input provided by the false surface would obviously be precise and crucial. This extreme kind of irony does of course occur, but it is not the only or even the most common type. The vital element in all literary irony is the presence of some signal to the reader that an apparent meaning must be modified; usually the signal implies that a truer meaning should then be found, or at least that the relationship among textual components needs to be reassessed. The ostensible signified must be rejected, and replaced by another signified which differs from it—at least slightly, and often radically—even though the 'same' signifier has sent us towards both possibilities. Meaning is often generated by the manner in which a particular surface leads us to a new reading.

The most famous and clearest case of irony in English literature is probably the first sentence in Jane Austen's *Pride and Prejudice*: 'It is a truth universally acknowledged, that a single man in possession of a good fortune must be in want of a wife'. An initial reading of this sentence in isolation discloses a grandiose but witty tone which might put us on our guard, whether or not we are familiar with or have expectations of Austen's way of working, yet the overt meaning still seems for the moment adequate (if a little unstable). By the time we reach the end of the novel's first page, however, it is already clear that this overt meaning requires some qualification. On a subsequent reading of the novel, the apparent meaning of its first sentence has become seriously inadequate. We might notice here, though, that the overt meaning must be sufficiently plausible that for the moment we can accept it as a possible primary meaning; and our reconstruction of the sentence's deeper significance can never completely demolish that initial reading. Moreover, the process by which we supplant (without fully replacing) an apparent with a truer significance can in itself become part of the sentence's meaning.

The 'truer' meaning of Austen's sentence, which its context shows unmistakably to be present and to displace the ostensible meaning in importance, can be formulated approximately as follows: 'It is a truth universally demonstrated, that when an ambitious woman with several daughters sees a single man in possession of a good fortune, she tries to make him marry one of her daughters.' In this case, our need to work out the meaning actually results from, and illustrates, the kind of deception initiated by Mrs Bennet within the novel's plot. The 'ostensible' meaning of the sentence really expresses her own rationalisation of her actions, and our reconstruction of the sentence's truer significance parallels Mr Bennet's demystification of his wife's schemes. We can easily imagine that Mrs Bennet has declared to her husband her conviction that 'everybody knows' a single man in possession of a good fortune must be in want of a wife. We can deduce, further, that Mr Bennet has realised how this formulation serves her as an ironic surface disguising the real motives for her matchmaking activities. In 'solving' the irony here, we are helped by our knowledge of what is to happen later in the plot; we possess this understanding when we re-read the novel. Mr Bennet acquires a similar kind of knowledge by observing the consistency with which Mrs Bennet repeats certain modes of scheming. Yet the fact that particular ironies will often affect the same reader in varying ways during different readings of a given text also suggests that irony may be partly directed towards a process of defamiliarising. Although we may feel rewarded with a sense of our own contribution to the understanding of a text when we have noticed an example of irony, many such examples work to resist our complacency, and instead remind us of the semantic and hermeneutic uncertainties which mark most texts.

In popular parlance, irony is often envisaged as a mode of judgment, frequently harsh judgment. The term may even appear loosely in conversation as a synonym for 'sarcasm'. In literary criticism, as well, irony is often envisaged primarily as a mode of judgment, as the expression of authorial hostility towards some component in a text. Hugh Kenner once claimed that 'irony is one-sided; it pushes the characters away from the author' (Kenner 1956: 23). Such authorial hostility may sometimes seem to be directed towards readers as well. Marilyn French, in her book on Joyce, discusses Northrop Frye's belief that in ironic writing an author 'turns his back on his audience' (French 111).

Yet a strikingly different popular usage also seems to have established itself recently: the use of the term 'irony' to denote an amusing discrepancy, often a discrepancy which highlights a person's folly or hypocrisy, but which is not in itself the product of human judgment. Indeed, in this usage, the less human intervention seems involved in a particular set of circumstances, the more insistently 'ironical' they are presumed to be. If this particular usage has indeed become common only in the later twentieth century—and earlier examples are difficult to find—its prevalence may well correlate with what is sometimes called a 'post-Christian' sensibility which envisages irony, rather than God or Providence, pulling the strings. People today will frequently label an occurrence 'ironical' which they or their predecessors might once have considered a striking or bizarre coincidence, an act of fate, or a sign of divine intervention.

Irony in literature, similarly, need not be judgmental or critical. Often it will appear not as the product of an author's specific message, but as a reflection of the way the world presented in the text is organised or goes about its business. Sometimes it will seem exactly the kind of 'cosmic irony' reflected in popular usage, and it will have the effect of suggesting that, the world being as it is, 'ironic' events must necessarily occur. In some cases a 'truer meaning' proves elusive or non-existent, and the need to reject the surface leads to considerable semantic insecurity, an insecurity which may in itself come to constitute—however paradoxically—a text's primary meaning. D. C. Muecke comments that, as Roland Barthes uses the term, 'irony' refers to 'a way of writing designed to leave open the question of what the literal meaning might signify: there is a perpetual deferment of significance. The old definition of irony—saying one thing and giving to understand the contrary—is superseded; irony is saying something in a way that activates not one but an endless series of subversive interpretations' (Muecke 31). Thus irony may, at times, work chiefly to demonstrate the instability of meaning. Its prevalence may then come to imply a recognition of 'instability' of other kinds as well, and especially of the potentially subversive role of the sign in any text.

Irony may well have changed its tone or enlarged its capabilities during the twentieth century. In *Irony/Humor: Critical Paradigms*, Candace D. Lang differentiates 'Romantic' or 'Modernist' irony, characterised by judgment, intentionality, and semantic or hermeneutic certainty, from 'Postmodernist' irony, characterised by textual self-consciousness and semantic or hermeneutic uncertainty. Lang argues that Postmodernist irony differs so radically from earlier forms that it should have a distinct name, and proposes 'humor' for this purpose. Such nomenclature seems problematic: the term 'humor' (humour) has other meanings and implications, and the variety of irony thus designated by Lang may not be 'humorous' in any of the everyday senses of the word. More importantly, the two types of irony Lang describes continue to resemble one another in their dependence on the disjunction of actual and apparent significance. Lang's distinction nonetheless seems essentially valid, but it may separate types of irony (or modes of reading) more profoundly than it separates historical phenomena. A precocious Romantic or

Modernist writer could use Lang's 'Postmodernist' irony. Joyce, surely, makes extensive use of both ironic types; sometimes he even manipulates the various kinds of interplay which may link them.

The prevalence of irony in any text must have semantic and thematic implications; and the more frequent the cases of irony, the more insistent these implications will become. Irony correlates with, and so helps to convey, the notion that the world offers no single meanings, only double or multiple ones; that any asserted, overt meaning hovers above alternatives to itself, and constantly threatens to collapse into them; that variety, relativism, and self-contradiction are inescapable phenomena. If any text operates as a system of differences, so does the world; and if an ironic text demonstrates that elements in a system may differ not only from other elements but from themselves, then it claims that the world works in a similar manner. As Bert O. States argues, 'what the ironist will always emphasize, in his eternal role as metaphysical heckler, is an unsuspected relatedness among things, the insufficiency of thinking you can have one thing without getting something not bargained for as well' (States 226).

Each participant in any situation in life or fiction, moreover, observes it from a particular viewpoint which is not shared by other witnesses, and an ironic text often sets out to illustrate such discrepancies in our angles of perception. Yet by illustrating and emphasising the discrepancies, by showing how we can all become aware of them, the ironic work may suggest a broader, less one-eyed perspective which brings us together. As Booth says, in ironic texts 'the building of amiable communities is often far more important than the exclusion of naive victims' (Booth 28). Many of the ironies to be discussed in this book establish positive associations and affinities which, without the presence of the irony, would remain unnoticed.

It is clear that irony requires considerable vigilance on the part of readers. Indeed, we might argue that an author who makes persistent use of irony may do so chiefly to ensure that a reader will remain actively involved in the creation of a text's meaning: to show that complex aesthetic or moral distinctions are in question and call for attention—quite the opposite of Frye's scenario in which writers turn their backs on readers. In an ironic text, the reader is challenged not merely to comprehend, but actually to reconsider and even to change the apparent connotations from moment to moment. Irony is thus one of the most demanding of all literary modes in terms of the obligation it places on the reader to engage, actively and alertly, in the interpretation of a text.

Irony could claim to be the most vital literary strategy employed by Joyce in particular. From his earliest writings to *Finnegans Wake*, but especially in the *Portrait* and *Ulysses*, the obliquities of irony suited many of his purposes. Irony helped him to avoid the direct address and didacticism which he always disliked, aided in the kind of indirect, ostensibly self-effacing moral judgment which he quickly came to prefer, and also lent itself to his fascination with words and their interpretation and misinterpretation. It proved helpful, furthermore, in the process of organising his books, especially through its remarkable flexibility of range and scale: an irony can remain local and precise, operating within a word or two, or it can expand to embrace a whole text, or its relationship to other texts or to the world at large. Irony may also be generated through the interplay among these sub-types, which sometimes operate in apparent antagonism to each other: particular displacements of meaning prompted by a local irony may be countermanded by other displacements which a broader ironic pattern seems in its turn to require.

Among other comparable literary devices, only metaphor operates so flexibly and so widely. Joyce employed metaphor extensively as well, but he found irony still more useful. These two devices, metaphor and irony, may be more closely associated than we usually think. Booth stresses that while irony often seems to discount the possible meanings which metaphor expresses, it also slyly affirms them. (It may be, indeed, that irony affirms such meanings all the more convincingly because in an ironic passage the alternative course of not affirming them has been so boldly and explicitly confronted.) Fritz Senn argues that irony is the 'core' of metaphor, since (in John Paul Riquelme's words) 'the attempt to produce equivalences also results in failures of fit' (Senn xix). Daniel R. Schwarz claims that 'metaphoricity—the making of comparisons—is a way of bringing together apparently dissimilar entities for the purpose of revealing resemblances and differences' (Schwarz 15); we could make precisely the same claim about many cases of irony.

Texts as radically ironic as Joyce's further emphasise the fact (or, at least, the assumption) that in literary interpretation there can never be a single 'correct' point of view. None of the meanings which we locate in his texts suffices completely to disprove or displace certain alternative connotations which also remain active. True meaning therefore arises from the coexistence, mingling or conflict of these alternative sub-meanings or discourses. The ultimate message of Joyce's text, then, must incorporate an assertion that the world is a collection of competing discourses, and a necessarily ironical place. Vicki Mahaffey makes the related point that Joyce's works 'accord with the theory that opposites are always and necessarily identical as well as different, a theory that posits value, not in one term of an opposition at the expense of the other, but in the continuing process of separation and reunion' (Mahaffey 4).

Joyce's affection for irony recalls his related fascination with ambiguity and with puns, with the experience of approximate congruity, with the phenomenon delineated in *Stephen Hero* as constituting 'an instant of all but union' (*SH* 199). As Richard Ellmann says, 'in a pun the component parts remain distinguishable, and yet there is a constant small excitement in their being yoked together so deftly and so improperly. . . . [Moreover] the pun extends beyond words. The same process goes on with people and incidents. A law of the Joycean universe is that every single thing is always on the verge of doubling with another' (Ellmann 1977: 90-91). Something similar could be said of ambiguity, especially as Joyce uses it, and of irony as well. In other words, every individual thing evokes, and stands poised over, something else which is congruous with it but also semantically discrete — often ironically so.

Irony, ambiguity and the pun may be usefully regarded as a continuum, rather than as three distinct entities. Occasionally, they may even overlap; for example, a pun might introduce or convey an ironic meaning. In all three cases there is an element of play, and in all three cases there is a single textual level which incorporates two or more semantic levels, so that the same words become capable of at least two readings. 'Judgment' is usually assumed to be common and crucial in irony, and possibly not present at all in ambiguity and the pun. In fact, it sometimes occurs in all three cases, but it need not be central in any of them.

A clearer distinction among the three forms might nevertheless be attempted. The pun always depends on a play of sound (occasionally supplemented or even displaced by visual analogies), and this kind of play will always be a crucial factor in our literary response; the pun may or may not have a 'primary' and a 'secondary' meaning. Ambiguity does not usually distinguish clearly between a primary and a secondary meaning and, in any case, one of its levels of meaning can never completely displace another level. (Some instances of 'irony' discussed in literary criticism involve concealed and overt meanings which remain almost equally viable; such cases might more usefully be regarded as examples of ambiguity.) Irony always has a primary and a secondary meaning; and when it functions successfully it tends to privilege the meaning which we reach after analysing the text, not the one we meet first.

Perhaps the only factor which always distinguishes puns and ambiguity from irony, then, is that in the case of irony there must be a hierarchy of preferences: one reading must be in some way superior to another. Moreover, the 'superior' reading will almost always be the initially 'concealed' one, not that which we first encounter as we approach the text. We might say that irony privileges its primary (initially concealed) meaning by 'de-privileging' its secondary (overt) meaning; and the primary meaning is also privileged by the efforts which readers have to make in the course of reconstructing and securing it.

Joyce's liking for these literary devices, and for irony in particular, has direct metaphysical implications. He seems constantly fascinated by the borderline between difference and similarity. He frequently asks at what precise point two phenomena come to resemble one another so closely that we see them as the same; or at what precise point two similar phenomena diverge so far that we see them as distinct from one another. Joyce, then, is intrigued by cases of 'all but union' because of the energy which they seem to derive from their sheer approximation; he shows a detective's delight in a world where things fail to fit neatly, and so betray themselves. Joyce sees the world as 'ironic' in a broad sense: as disjunctive, accidental, relativistic, yet inevitably linked together by often perverse associations, and open to cautious value judgments, if only in the form of the relativist's preference for one thing over another. To reflect this world, his texts must assume cognate—at least, approximately cognate—ironic contours.

One further, specific type of 'approximate union' which helps to shape *Ulysses* derives from Joyce's use of 'Homeric' material, and other material drawn from previous literature. Joyce manipulates a complex relationship, involving both resemblances and contrasts, between the world of Odysseus and the world of Leopold Bloom. There are various less central instances of such patterns, as in the relationship between Shakespeare's Hamlet and Joyce's Stephen Dedalus, the pattern being further complicated in this case by Stephen's own conscious awareness and exploitation of the association. In using such relationships in his novel Joyce expands the possibilities provided by puns, ambiguity and irony into larger schemes and patterns which colour much of the text.

Careful attention to Joyce's ways of using irony can often refine interpretations of his novel. For years, some readers have believed that *Ulysses* displays certain phenomena — particular themes, motifs or emphases — for whose presence little objective evidence actually exists. Such readers often overlook other phenomena which are more obviously or demonstrably present. Various critics have confidently intuited components necessary to their own readings, and slighted others which suited them less well. An early instance of this kind of critic was T. S. Eliot, who found in *Ulysses* a study of the futility of the contemporary world eerily akin to that conveyed in his own work, something which few readers of *Ulysses* now believe the novel to contain, except perhaps as a minor theme. In the process of presenting his analysis, Eliot virtually ignored the extreme stylistic variousness of *Ulysses*, which for many later critics seems by far its most striking and important characteristic. Until recently many readers believed that the novel's characters witnessed all the so-called 'hallucinations' in the 'Circe' episode, an interpretation which now seems almost impossible to sustain, and slighted the remarkable way in which these hallucinations, if that is what they are, happen exclusively or primarily to readers, who cannot even claim to be present in the text.

Years of earnest critical activity have yielded the now widely accepted conclusion that the list of Molly's 'lovers' which flits through Bloom's mind in 'Ithaca' represents Bloom's 'fears' or 'suspicions' rather than an account of Molly's actual sexual conquests. The novel abounds in evidence that Boylan is the first and only extramarital lover Molly has had, and given Bloom's decade of neglect of Molly, she should, realistically, be seen as exceptionally faithful to him, rather than the reverse. (Admittedly, much of the evidence for the details of Molly's sex life is concentrated in the 'Penelope' episode which follows 'Ithaca' and ends the

novel; but for Joyce this sequence is a typically ironic illustration of the need to avoid hasty judgments and to consider
all relevant discourses—in this case, Molly's discourse as well
as Bloom's—rather than seizing on any one discourse or
explanation as definitive.) Thus the irony which for decades
compelled many critics to see Molly as an unfaithful parody
of Penelope becomes double-edged, rebounding on those
critics who rushed to judgment. Adaline Glasheen cites some
examples of such precipitate criticism: Harry Levin claimed of
Molly in 1941 that 'twenty-five others have shared her bed
with Bloom'; Edmund Wilson remarked seven years later that
'[Mrs Bloom has] a prodigious sexual appetite'; and Mitchell
Morse added in 1959 that Molly 'has had a long series of
lovers. . . . She is a dirty joke' (Hart and Hayman 55). Phillip
F. Herring remarks that 'one is struck with the obvious irony
of Joyce's using Penelope as one of the models for Molly
Bloom. Penelope is a kind of paragon of wifely fidelity; Molly
seems to have an insatiable appetite for adultery' (Herring
1969: 53). Molly is, in fact, much more faithful than such
critics ever acknowledged, and Joyce's irony here serves as a
means of averting, not encouraging, harsh or simplistic
judgments.

Yet even to see the list as expressing Bloom's 'suspicions',
as some readers and critics still do, seems pedantic and
inappropriate. The list includes a few men whom Bloom may
indeed 'suspect', though we should remember that Bloom
feels particularly vulnerable at the moment when he draws
up the list because Molly has been to bed with Boylan earlier
in the day. Bloom's obvious suffering over this indisputable
fact may make him momentarily suspicious of almost any
man who has ever been near Molly. But much more conspicuous in the list are men who, Bloom must know perfectly
well, have had no sexual contact whatever with Molly
beyond seeing her in the street and possibly thinking her
attractive. Many of them can have been no closer to Molly
than Bloom was to the woman he watched across the street in
'Lotus Eaters' in the frustrated hope of seeing her stockings;

and Bloom's 'involvement' with Gerty MacDowell in the 'Nausicaa' episode probably surpasses in sensual intimacy Molly's contact with any of the men, other than Boylan, appearing in Bloom's catalogue. This comparison between the sexual endeavours of the two Blooms juxtaposes one day in Leopold Bloom's life (admittedly a day on which he felt a particularly strong need of sexual consolation) with more than a decade in Molly's life. The list of 'lovers' should be seen, in the main, as Bloom's partly troubled and partly amused comment on the ubiquity of human sexual impulses. More seriously, it suggests Bloom's unfair attempt to label Molly as promiscuous, for his own benefit or for ours. It is a rather successful attempt, if earlier critics' responses to the text are to be trusted. As Glasheen says, 'that Bloom is a very believable man is sufficiently proved by the simple faith with which readers . . . used to accept as real the twenty-six lovers for which Bloom . . . forgives Molly' (Hart and Hayman 55).

Perhaps readers should even cultivate more scepticism about some of the naturalistic events apparently recounted in *Ulysses* which have always been accepted as authentic. There are passages of directly quoted speech in 'Circe' and elsewhere (notably in 'Eumaeus') which can hardly have been spoken as they appear. Most of the information we receive about Molly Bloom's past appears highly dubious. We might even wonder whether the soldier, Private Carr, actually knocks Stephen down. To be knocked down in the street by a 'Private Carr' seems a curious fate for him, and we might wonder whether some kind of pun is intended; but as Joyce reminds us in *Finnegans Wake*, 'you cannot make a limousine lady out of a hillman minx' (*FW* 376).

Some critics speak persistently about a 'narrator' in *Ulysses*, or about a pair or series of narrators. Granted, few critics go to the anthropomorphic extreme of envisaging these figures as real people, though Kenner confidently succeeds in finding what he calls a Vivid Narrator and a Second Narrator, the latter akin, he says, to the 'harsh and awkward' narrator envisaged by Clive Hart (Kenner 1978: 104). Kenner remarks of a particular passage in the 'Hades' episode that 'the Arranger, we may guess, arranged those sentences, snatching the pen from his anonymous colleague' (Kenner 1980: 67). French detects in *Ulysses* a palpable rogues' gallery of narrative presences (French, *passim*). Yet even as a metaphor the term 'narrator' may be misleading. Joyce scarcely alludes to a narrator in his own discussions of the writing of *Ulysses*, and his personal conception of the novel's machinery may have been entirely different. The recently established critical term 'discourse' (not that Joyce used this term either) seems more appropriate, in its simultaneous neutrality and specificity, to Joyce's way of writing. We need not assign to a given discourse a full set of personal characteristics such as a 'narrator' seems required by definition to possess. Also, the coexistence of numerous discourses—modes of thought, speech, description, evaluation—in *Ulysses* seems indisputable, while the value of intuiting narrative personae in the novel appears increasingly dubious.

Irony is a still more neutral (but also more specific) critical term which, in the context of *Ulysses*, covers ground similar to that claimed by the advocates of narrators and discourses. The phenomenon of competing narrators or competing discourses is necessarily an ironical one, since it requires readers to query a surface meaning and seek alternatives to it, alternatives which may sometimes seem in the text to be the words of another narrator or those of another discourse. Much of the energy of *Ulysses* works to dispel the notion that a single overarching mode of address will ever be capable of spanning the multiple disjunctions created by its range of competing discourses. As Colin MacCabe puts it, 'none of the discourses which circulate in . . . *Ulysses* can master or make sense of the others' (MacCabe 14).

A form of irony which Joyce particularly enjoyed involves the wide separation, in a text, of the ironic components—the textual elements whose juxtaposition in our minds is necessary to establish ironic meaning. It sometimes seems that Joyce preferred these components to be placed as far apart as possible, presumably to increase the effort required to bring them together, and the consequent impact which results once the pattern is noticed. Thus we find in *Ulysses* many intriguing cases where a passage's apparently adequate, self-enclosed meaning is only revealed as ironic—only revealed, that is, as 'chiefly signifying something else'—when another, geographically quite distant, passage in the novel is brought near to it in our imagination.

Besides ironies which connect neighbouring or widely separated points within *Ulysses* itself, Joyce also exploits ironic associations linking passages in the novel with various external locations, associations which help fix or enrich the meaning of his text. Such locations include his own earlier works, especially *A Portrait of the Artist as a Young Man*, but also *Dubliners* and *Exiles*; the works of other authors, notably Shakespeare's *Hamlet* and Homer's *Odyssey*; and extra-literary aspects of the real world, including geographical details of the actual Dublin. In all these cases, our full response to the meaning of a passage in *Ulysses* requires knowledge of such external locations and the ironic discrepancies or other ironic associations which Joyce establishes between the external location and an allusion to it presented within *Ulysses* itself.

This study will investigate such ironic modes in sequence, beginning with the most immediate, and moving to those which involve the widest apparent gap between the text and the other term of a particular ironic transaction. The second chapter analyses 'local' ironies—those which operate chiefly within individual words, sentences or paragraphs. Examples will be drawn from 'Telemachus', 'Eumaeus' and 'Penelope' in particular; in all these episodes, irony is crucial to meaning but is partly shrouded in the deliberate strangeness of Joyce's style. The third chapter considers those ironies which move from page to page but are largely confined to a single episode. Detailed studies will be made here of 'Wandering Rocks' and 'Ithaca'. Both episodes convey an appearance of rigorous precision, which Joyce carefully undermines for his own ironic purposes. In the fourth chapter, inter-episode ironies are considered — those which work chiefly to link one episode with another. The associations between 'Proteus' and 'Nausicaa' serve as a paradigmatic example of inter-episode irony.

The fifth chapter moves to ironies which link *Ulysses* with Joyce's previous texts, particular attention being paid to associations between the *Portrait* and the first three episodes of *Ulysses*. These episodes ironically qualify the impression of Stephen which we receive at the end of the *Portrait*. The association between the *Portrait* and the 'Nausicaa' episode will also be discussed here. Then, in the sixth chapter, ironic links between *Ulysses* and certain texts by other authors are explored, with the *Odyssey* and *Hamlet* serving as the principal examples. These ironies are designed to elicit subtle responses from readers to Joyce's text; they do not aim to show the inferiority of Joyce's characters to their Homeric or Shakespearean predecessors. The seventh chapter studies ironic links with the 'real world' of historical facts, noting Joyce's use of such documented extra-textual realities as his own biographical circumstances, the geography of Dublin, and the history of Ireland. Here again, Joyce's aim in using such ironies is not to limit his characters, but to enhance our response to them. Finally, the eighth chapter considers the ironic interplay which Joyce sets up among the various ironic modes discussed in the preceding chapters, and the effects of that interplay.

Attention is also paid, in this concluding chapter, to Joyce's own views of the literary uses of irony. Ironic modes seem central in almost all Joyce's acts of communication — except, perhaps, in some of his letters and some of his poems. His pronouncements on literary matters are especially marked by irony, and nowhere more so than when he touches on the subject of irony itself. The master of ironic modes can hardly be expected to speak directly about the topic: such an approach would be almost a contradiction in terms. His essay 'A Portrait of the Artist', written in 1904 but not published during his lifetime, is largely an account of his own artistic development to date. In this text Joyce includes the bold claim: 'Mastery of art had been achieved in irony' (*P* 263). Though the context of the claim remains cryptic and no clear aesthetic or philosophical conclusions appear, the centrality of irony has nonetheless, for a brief moment, been declared. Joyce never addressed the topic so explicitly again.

2
Local Ironies

The 'local ironies' of *Ulysses*—those which operate chiefly within a word, phrase, sentence or paragraph—are the most pervasive, conspicuous and insistent ironies in the novel. To catalogue them all would require a book far longer than the novel itself. The local ironies are also the most diverse in their ways of operation. For these reasons, this chapter cannot hope to study such ironies comprehensively. To do so would, in any case, divert disproportionate attention to them, since certain other modes, while less frequently represented in the text, often work more radically than the local instances. Rather, this chapter will investigate some typical cases of local irony, then analyse at greater length a few episodes which seem especially dependent on such ironies, or which make especially interesting use of them—essentially, 'Telemachus', 'Eumaeus' and 'Penelope'.

Ulysses contains thousands of instances of ironic phrasing. Some such examples might be better classified as ambiguities or puns, but many remain primarily ironical in the terms proposed for this study. In other words, the more significant meaning is the initially concealed one, and irony privileges this meaning by 'de-privileging' its secondary (overt) counterpart. Sometimes, the interplay between the overt and concealed meanings contributes further important connotations to the novel. In every case, we return to the surface of the text armed with a new and deeper awareness of semantic possibilities.

In the 'Nausicaa' episode Bloom, meditating quietly after the climax of his encounter with Gerty MacDowell, reflects 'Ten bob I got for Molly's combings when we were on the rocks in Holles street' (13/840-41). The phrase 'on the rocks'

will strike most readers initially as a common English metaphorical idiom meaning 'in difficulties' or 'in danger of
(financial) insolvency'. But Bloom happens to be sitting on a
rock as this thought crosses his mind; thus the idiom,
becoming literal, necessarily invokes his present context
(unconsciously, it seems) as well as recalling his past life
consciously, and prompts readers to notice associations
between the two situations, associations which may not be
fully apparent to Bloom himself. In the present scene, Bloom
appears to be 'on the rocks' metaphorically as well as literally,
and while his financial position may not be under direct
threat, as it was in the Holles street days, the stability of his
household seems more tenuous now than it had been then.
Bloom's last action before the phrase 'on the rocks' appears in
the text, his self-stimulation while ogling Gerty, reminds us
that his marriage may now be 'on the rocks' and that his
strategies for coping with this problem include a measure of
mere evasiveness. Since Bloom is sitting not merely on a rock
but at a beach, the metaphor seems to be further literalised,
and we can readily imagine the 'shipwreck' of his personal or
marital fortunes. An additional layer of ironic suggestion
appears if we detect an allusion to Odysseus, that mariner
who is famous for his bravery but whose resourcefulness and
courage nevertheless fail on several occasions to keep him
safe from shipwreck and rocks. (We may also hear a faint
echo of Molly's remark to Bloom in 'Calypso', when she
makes a negative judgment on his admittedly ineffectual
attempts to explain the word 'metempsychosis': 'O, rocks!' [4/
343]. Bloom has, in turn, recalled Molly's comment, with
implicit acceptance of her wariness about abstraction, in
'Sirens': 'Philosophy. O rocks!' [11/1062]. These earlier passages, if we link them to the one in 'Nausicaa', considerably
enrich its implications for the Blooms' relationship.) That the
phrase used in 'Nausicaa' seemed important and apposite to
Joyce may be confirmed from its appearance in several of his
letters, such as the one he wrote to Frank Budgen on 7

November 1919, where he remarks: 'As for *Ulysses* — it is like me — on the rocks' (*L I* 130).

A few lines after his recollection of life at Holles street, we hear that 'Mr Bloom with careful hand recomposed his wet shirt' (13/851). The overt meaning of this sentence seems momentarily sufficient, the slightly precious term 'recomposed' apparently chosen to reinforce the impression of Bloom's sedately post-orgasmic action. Yet further connotations for the sentence quickly suggest themselves: 'careful' reasserts its (etymologically prior but now less common) implication 'burdened with cares' rather than 'skilful' or 'heedful'. The word 'recomposed' hints at Bloom's retrieval of his earlier composure; it also seems to invoke the creation and revision of works of art, especially literary texts, as well as designating Bloom's rearrangement of his moist clothing. We are thus led from the immediate setting and action to reflect on Bloom's emotional state, and perhaps also on associations between Bloom and the creation of the text in which he appears.

'Scylla and Charybdis', an episode much concerned with language, with debate among conflicting points of view and with the problem of appearance and reality, makes apt and extensive use of local irony. Several instances help to convey the personalities of the poet AE and the library staff, literary or quasi-literary figures who serve as a chorus for Stephen's earnest disquisition, and whose attributes focus our attention on the same question of the disjunctiveness of art and life that dominates Stephen's discussion of Shakespeare. Several ironic contrasts distinguish Stephen's expansive view of the artist's response to experience from the attenuated lives of AE, John Eglinton, Richard Best and Thomas Lyster. This pattern is unwittingly established by the 'urbane' librarian Lyster in the episode's opening lines. Alluding to Shakespeare's *Hamlet* and Goethe's *Wilhelm Meister*, he evokes 'a hesitating soul taking arms against a sea of troubles, torn by conflicting doubts, as one sees in real life' (9/3-4). We doubt whether the librarian and his colleagues have much contact with 'real life' as Joyce might define it, and this doubt is clearly shared by Stephen and embodied in the narrative manner. Stephen thinks of the library staff members: 'unwed, unfancied, ware of wiles, they fingerponder nightly each his variorum edition of *The Taming of the Shrew*' (9/1062-3). Here the implications of aloofness, sterility, masturbation, misogyny and perhaps homosexuality are clearly intended by Stephen and endorsed by the narrative, not that Stephen feels actively hostile to the librarians—for the moment he shares their urbanity, or appears to do so. But they inevitably form a somewhat antagonistic audience, since their personalities and attitudes align them in opposition to Stephen's argument. In this respect they recall Stephen's associates Davin, Lynch and Cranly in the *Portrait*, each of whom challenges Stephen by embodying views opposed to his on the particular subject which their respective conversation chiefly treats (essentially, patriotism with Davin, art with Lynch and personal relationships with Cranly). More profound ironies also mark 'Scylla and Charybdis', but they mostly work by contrasting the episode with other parts of the novel and with Shakespeare, and will be considered later.

When Joyce added the 'headlines' (or 'captions') to the 'Aeolus' episode, he strongly accentuated the self-referential quality of the text of *Ulysses* and our awareness of this quality. Most of the headlines react ironically with the narrative surrounding them. As Karen Lawrence observes, in this episode 'the book turns back on itself to comment on and parody its own assumptions, explicitly in the way the headings "comment" on or rewrite the micro-narrative and implicitly in the way the chapter exceeds and incorporates the novel we have read in the early chapters. Although the plot continues, the novel begins a radical questioning of the authority of its writing' (Lawrence 59). 'Aeolus' thus helps to prepare readers for the narrative dislocations and ironic disjunctions of the later episodes. In addition, it helps us to notice on subsequent readings of the novel that these features also appear in the episodes which precede 'Aeolus' in the text. The novel contains numerous seemingly casual hints about its own modes of operation and, consequently, about the modes of reading which it requires. Bloom points out in 'Eumaeus', while evaluating the tales told by 'Murphy' in the cabman's shelter, that 'analogous scenes are occasionally, if not often, met with' (16/849). Bloom's comment reminds us of the oblique and disjunctive manner of *Ulysses*, and of our consequent obligation to find internal 'analogies' in the text which may help our reading to cohere. Patrick A. McCarthy, in his essay '*Ulysses* and the Printed Page', finds a similar involution in Martha Clifford's letter, read by Bloom in the 'Lotus Eaters' episode:

> While its short sentences, sterling phrasing, and limited vocabulary seem to place [Martha's] letter at the opposite end of the literary spectrum from *Ulysses* as a whole, there are several signs that the letter, like other written or printed documents, is a microcosm of the book: the unimaginative repetition of phrases (Dear Henry, Henry dear; naughty boy, naughty darling) and the tendency to circle back to the same idea (punishment, the demand that he write, their future meeting) parody Joyce's use of repeated themes and images to unify and lend meaning to his novel.
>
> (Newman and Thornton 68)

'Telemachus' abounds in local irony. Since this episode begins the novel, it obviously cannot contain allusions to preceding portions of the text, as do all its successors. Allusions to subsequent episodes, though in *Ulysses* Joyce employs such forward-looking allusions more persistently than do most authors, also seem scarce in 'Telemachus'. References to the *Portrait* occur, but not overwhelmingly. While ironic allusions to Homer and to the realm of 'external fact' also appear in the text of this episode, they seldom seem central to interpretation, and a reader encountering *Ulysses* for the first time cannot expect to know how best to react to them. For all these (largely structural) reasons, the irony of 'Telemachus' tends to work chiefly in a local and self-enclosed manner.

The episode, however, also emphasises the concept of self-enclosure in more directly thematic ways, which Joyce's concentration on this mode of irony may serve primarily to accentuate. Stephen's sense of circumstantial entrapment — in his poverty, in Ireland and with Buck Mulligan — is frequently paralleled and highlighted by the episode's imagery. Numerous objects and settings appear in a configuration which emphasises their power to enclose or entrap: the tower itself, and both the walled tower-top and the hell-like, internal living quarters; Dublin bay; the forty-foot swimming hole; the 'niche' where the priest dresses. Stephen peers myopically and ineffectually at the world around him, and life at the tower appears to be a closed system. Thus it seems appropriate that the episode's irony should be predominantly local.

Much of Stephen's sense of confinement in 'Telemachus' seems to be caused by, or at least focused on, Mulligan. He appears as a usurper, especially in Stephen's eyes, but also as a gaoler, a role symbolised by his insistence on retaining possession of the key to the tower. He seeks to take over, and thus to curtail and trammel, Stephen's self-perceived role as a creative verbal artist, a priest of eternal imagination. A speech of Mulligan's, we hear, is made 'frankly' (1/51), but the adverb reflects little more than his posturing self-image: the speech in question is not frank but disingenuous and even hostile. His supposedly 'frank' remark, made to Stephen about Haines, is 'God, isn't he dreadful? . . . He thinks you're not a gentleman' (1/51-2). In reality, Mulligan aligns himself with Haines, labels him 'dreadful' mostly in order to mock Stephen obliquely, and masks his own view that Stephen is 'not a gentleman' by attributing it to Haines (who may well share it, but whose opinions have little substance away from Mulligan's influence, as Mulligan knows perfectly well). That the ironic reference to frankness reflects Mulligan's own self-estimate seems confirmed a little later. He accosts Stephen: 'Why don't you trust me more? What have you up your nose against me? . . . Cough it up. I'm quite frank with you. What have you against me now?' (1/161-2; 1/179-80). Here the claim of frankness again masks insincerity. The imagery also operates ironically; an obvious physiological disjunction, which has oddly been devised by Mulligan the medical student, mars the logic of the sequence of phrases 'What have you up your nose against me?' and 'Cough it up', which follow one another in his argument and are separated by only 17 lines of text. Stephen's gesture of picking his nose at the end of 'Proteus' recalls Mulligan's comment (and may suggest, wryly and modestly, the possibility of Stephen's liberation). The phrase 'Cough it up' may be randomly chosen by Mulligan, but it nonetheless vividly evokes for Stephen his troubled reflections about his mother's death (her final illness being characterised by the vomiting of bile), a subject which already preoccupies Stephen and which he now proceeds to discuss, earnestly and painfully. His distress over Mulligan's disingenuousness and hypocrisy seems strongest when he recalls the occasion of his mother's death and Mulligan's insensitivity at that time. Mulligan's bland statement 'The aunt thinks you killed your mother' (1/88) subtly but cruelly suggests, in its application of the definite article to his own relation and the personal pronoun to Stephen's, that personal attachments like Stephen's feeling for his mother are sentimental indulgences.

The clash of viewpoints dividing Stephen and Mulligan marks the episode (and hence the novel) from the beginning, and irony becomes the principal means of conveying this clash. Mulligan's pretence of enacting a black mass establishes an ironic tone at the outset, since a black mass is always an ironic formal parody, and since Mulligan's assumption of the quasi-priestly role of black-mass celebrant stresses his usurping disposition. Mulligan also complicates an innocent reader's response to *Ulysses*, a novel with a conspicuously 'classical' title, by producing the text's first spoken words, in Latin—'*Introibo ad altare Dei*' (1/5), and prompting the text's first fragment of interior monologue, in Greek—'Chrysostomos' (1/26). Both instances are parodic and ironic: the first phrase, from the Latin Mass, is spoken by Mulligan in a mocking manner as he ascends to the tower-top rather than to the altar; the Greek word, meaning 'golden-mouthed' and denoting a Church Father, is used by Stephen as a critical comment on Mulligan's glib sense of priestly superiority and its actual, mundane dependence on financial solidity (Mulligan's teeth shine with expensive gold fillings, while Stephen's are rotting). Mulligan continues to mock classical precedents, and our expectation of their importance to *Ulysses*, by alluding to Stephen's 'absurd name, an ancient Greek!' (1/34) and attributing a 'Hellenic ring' to his own name (1/42). He even suggests, with obvious insincerity, that he and Stephen might embark on a shared visit to Greece—a false trail for a reader in quest of Odyssean developments in *Ulysses* (1/42-3). We might also notice that during this 'conversation', Mulligan speaks eight times before Stephen has a chance to say anything.

The episode's first two words—'stately' and 'plump'— stress the disjunction between the two characters and their attitudes: Buck Mulligan might regard himself as 'stately', but never as 'plump'. Yet in the ironic context of 'Telemachus' the term 'stately' also takes on connotations which Mulligan would not welcome; notably, it suggests (accurately) that he is an accomplice of the state, a conservative whose declared radicalism is all affectation. Such connotations (and the view that Mulligan is 'plump') could only be supplied by another witness, who in the present context must be Stephen Dedalus. Stephen first appears in the text several lines after Mulligan, a sequence which evokes Buck's dominance. Stephen is described as 'displeased and sleepy' (1/13), a phrase which contrasts with the application to Mulligan of the adjective 'pleasant' (1/33) and the adverb 'pleasantly' (1/379), and tends to cling to him since it alliterates with his full name, which has appeared twice in three lines and once in conjunction with the phrase in question: 'Stephen Dedalus, displeased and sleepy' (1/13). In the next few lines we hear more explicitly his view of his companion: Stephen 'looked coldly at the shaking gurgling face that blessed him, equine in its length, and at the light untonsured hair, grained and hued like pale oak' (1/14-16). These lines repudiate the notion of Mulligan as a priest, which Buck is busily if facetiously promulgating, and liken him rather to an animal and a tree. Ironically, Mulligan seems to retaliate later by applying similar imagery to Stephen: 'You put your hoof in it now' (1/496). Another description of Mulligan, 'Laughter seized all his strong wellknit trunk' (1/132-3), appears to evoke Mulligan's self-image; but it also recalls for us Stephen's use of the simile of the tree.

The narrative of 'Telemachus' undermines Mulligan's self-image further by surrounding him with distorted patterns of imagery. Most frequently, personification attributes human traits to the inanimate objects with which he deals, like his 'rebellious tie' (1/513) and the grasses and ferns to which he talks (1/536). We also hear of his 'talking hands' (1/518), and at times his voice seems disembodied: 'Buck Mulligan's voice sang from within the tower. It came nearer up the staircase, calling again' (1/281-2). (The text treats Haines's voice in the same way [1/666], thus emphasising the point about disembodied expression, as well as accentuating the affinity between Haines and Mulligan.) These passages ironically evoke Mulligan's awkward and sometimes brutish relationship with his environment. He seems a man of surfaces and costumes: we hear that he 'put on' a smiling face (1/579), so assuming a mask. He spends much of the episode dressing (grandly, vainly) or undressing again (very soon after, and a few yards away) in order to swim. His desired attire of 'puce gloves and green boots' (1/516) seems decadent, and self-contradictory in its simultaneous symbolic evocation of both England and Ireland. Mulligan even quotes Walt Whitman in a wry confession of this trait: 'Do I contradict myself? Very well then, I contradict myself' (1/517). But Mulligan's blithe awareness and acknowledgment of his own contradictions does not disguise them, prevent them from being contradictions, or render them harmless.

Much of the irony in 'Eumaeus' also operates chiefly on a local scale. Like 'Telemachus', this episode serves as the beginning both of a triad of episodes and of one of the novel's three main sections. The first two lines of 'Eumaeus' allude insistently to the characters and events of 'Telemachus', thus reinforcing the pattern: the words 'brushed', 'shavings' and 'bucked' recall Buck Mulligan's shaving scene on the novel's first page. Bloom's brushing off the 'greater bulk' (16/1) of the shavings from the prone (and ill-nourished) Stephen may even recall for a reader the 'greater bulk' of Mulligan's 'stately, plump' form (1/1). Mahaffey notes that 'structurally, the "*soi-disant* sailor" who styles himself Murphy is the counterpart of Mulligan, just as "Eumaeus" mirrors "Telemachus" in the tripartite structure of *Ulysses*. . . . Whereas Mulligan regards appearances as purely exterior, changing his "clothing" whenever there is advantage in doing so, Murphy wears a human face *beneath* his clothing, indelibly imprinted on his skin' (Mahaffey 172). With a few such exceptions, however, Joyce seems in 'Eumaeus' to limit his allusions to previous episodes, in part to focus attention on the immediate situation and its implications for the material that is to follow it. Aptly enough, in these terms, the episode's opening phrase is 'Preparatory to anything else' (16/1). Although 'Eumaeus' appears as the sixteenth of the novel's eighteen episodes, much of its purpose is indeed preparatory, rather than recapitulative.

As in the case of 'Telemachus', thematic aspects of 'Eumaeus' both make the deployment of local irony appropriate and profit from its presence. The cabman's shelter serves literally as a refuge after the wildness of 'Circe'; some of the shelter's inhabitants may be unsavoury, but none seems dangerous, and Bloom gains a welcome opportunity to catch his breath and to make an attempt at showing solicitude for

Stephen. When Bloom and Stephen eventually leave the cabman's shelter, they make for another relatively sheltered environment, Bloom's own house. To some extent, then, stasis and self-enclosure are appropriately privileged in 'Eumaeus'. The whole episode, in fact, seems self-enclosed. Elsewhere in the novel, puzzles and problems tend to be solved, if at all, by reference to other episodes, but in 'Eumaeus' the solutions, if any, tend to appear within the text of the episode. John Gordon comments that 'in his schema, Joyce designated "nerves" as the "organ" of the episode, not, it should be stressed, the nervous system: concentrated points of attention, not the network connecting them' (Gordon 115). In this instance, the schema seems an apt correlative of the episode's operations. Though the episode's self-enclosed irony partly reflects the tired state of the central characters, their reluctance to range widely in intellectual matters or otherwise, it also demonstrates the degree of resourcefulness which both of them (especially Bloom) can sometimes attain even in difficult circumstances. Stephen still seems to feel threatened by enclosed spaces, but those which surround him in 'Eumaeus' clearly trouble him less than those whose effects he suffered in 'Telemachus'.

While critical readings of 'Eumaeus' routinely stress the affinities between its dominant moods and Bloom's own sensibility, it might be more accurate to associate those moods with the episode's general situation. Bloom partakes of this situation with a greater sense of accomplishment (bordering occasionally on triumph) than anyone else present in the episode, and some affinities with his state of mind do therefore exist. But various parts of the narrative seem closer in mood to the consciousnesses of Stephen—Murphy, the anonymous keeper of the shelter, even the city at night—and Bloom's centrality often appears under threat. Many of the episode's ironies, indeed, serve to show the limitations in Bloom's personality, situation, or sense of context which precipitate such threats to his autonomy. Frequent ironic disjunctions drive a wedge between Bloom's perceptions and those which are apparently endorsed by the episode's narrative.

'Eumaeus' shows a persistent ironic gap between matter and manner. Many of the other late episodes of *Ulysses* also explore the problematic relationship of form and content, but in 'Eumaeus', more consistently than in any other episode, the disjunction takes the form of a contrast between slender events and wordy, overstated means of presenting (or sometimes obscuring) those events. The text demonstrates that our freedom to select any verbal construction—with no limit to the time available for undertaking this operation—cannot guarantee clarity, logic or the conquest of ambiguity. The semantic uncertainty which irony always involves thus becomes directly thematic here.

A clear (and delightful) example of such semantic uncertainty is provided by the newspaper account of the Dignam funeral, which for our benefit appears in full within the text of 'Eumaeus' as Bloom reads it quietly to himself. Bloom, we learn, is 'nettled' by the newspaper's spelling of his name as 'L. Boom' (16/1262). This error seems at first to represent merely an inadvertent slip by the reporter or compositor, but it also conveys, accurately enough, a widespread Dublin carelessness about Bloom's sense of his own identity. Moreover, it distorts his surname by the omission of a letter, as if seeking to reduce him, and seems to transfer that letter in a clumsy attempt to furnish him with a first initial. All the other mourners who were present at Dignam's graveside are identified in the report by first name as well as surname, and we recall that in 'Hades' they mostly addressed one another, but not Bloom, by first name. At the funeral, reporter Hynes had tactlessly asked Bloom, 'What is your christian name? I'm not sure' (6/880-81). It seems that he paid attention only to the first portion of Bloom's reply: 'L, Mr Bloom said. Leopold' (6/882). Bloom feels further, more professionally, 'nettled' by a line of garbled type in the report (caused by a lapse in the compositor's attention). But he is said to be 'tickled to death' (16/1263)—an appropriate phrase in the context of an account of a funeral—by three other errors of inclusion or mis-identification: 'C. P. M'Coy and Stephen Dedalus B. A. who were conspicuous, needless to say, by their total absence (to say nothing of M'Intosh)' (16/1263-5). The appearance of M'Coy's name, with initials only, seems to align him in the list with Bloom, similarly designated, even though Bloom had actually been present at the funeral while M'Coy had not; and M'Coy only appears in the list at all because Bloom had supplied his name to the reporter. We learn that Hynes knows M'Coy's full name, and thus has seemingly chosen not to use it. Bloom had made the request: 'You might put down M'Coy's name too. He asked me to', to which Hynes had responded: '—Charley, Hynes said writing. I know. He was on the *Freeman* once' (6/882-4). But in M'Coy's case (unlike Bloom's) the newspaper prints the name in the form its owner seemingly prefers and had specified, even though Bloom apparently failed to convey that specification explicitly to Hynes; in 'Lotus Eaters' M'Coy had remarked to Bloom 'Just C. P. M'Coy will do' (5/176). The newspaper's inclusion of absent Stephen's full name (to say nothing of the allusion to his academic qualifications) might seem a further inadvertent insult to Bloom, though fortunately he chooses instead to find the reference amusing.

Thus the narrative of 'Eumaeus', assimilating for a moment the actual words of the newspaper report, reminds us of the potential unreliability of all texts. The next few lines of narrative in *Ulysses* also seem contaminated by the newspaper story: 'L. Boom pointed it out to his companion B. A. engaged in stifling another yawn, half nervousness, not forgetting the usual crop of nonsensical howlers of misprints' (16/1265-7). A few lines later Bloom acquires more explicitly 'for the nonce his new misnomer' (16/1274-5). Here Bloom and Stephen seem momentarily confined to the slender degree of reality which the newspaper had bestowed on them; the phrase 'his companion B. A.', for example, depends on the newspaper's identification of Stephen by the irrelevant allusion to academic qualifications and its erroneous implication that Stephen had been at the funeral as a 'companion' of Bloom.

The newspaper account—depicting an event which *Ulysses* has already narrated for us in an earlier episode—implies that we should be correspondingly wary about the textual surface of the novel itself, correspondingly alert to nuances conveyed by textual disturbances like local irony. 'Eumaeus', in particular, appears throughout to derive idioms from Irish provincial newspapers, as Kenner suggests (Kenner 1980: 131). Joyce showed himself to be a critic and connoisseur of such literary modes as early as 1907, in his lecture on James Clarence Mangan. Here he claims that Mangan's 'essays in prose are perhaps interesting on the first reading, but, in truth, they are insipid attempts. The style is conceited, in the worst sense of the word, strained, and banal, the subject trivial and inflated, the kind of prose, in fact, in which the bits of local news are written in a bad rural newspaper' (*CW* 182). It therefore seems appropriate that 'Eumaeus' should contain an explicit warning about the unreliability of newspaper discourse. This emphasis also reminds us that Bloom often depends on such bland, tepid public idioms as that of the newspaper in order to express himself—partly, no doubt, because he works for a newspaper and in the advertising field, but perhaps also as a mark of his self-effacing modesty and his occasional anxious desire to become less marginal, more accepted by society. Perhaps unconsciously, he accepts the discourse of the newspaper as equivalent to the discourse of the community. We know from his interior monologue that Bloom has interesting and original thoughts, but few of them ever reach the surface of his speech. Bloom's outwardly professed political credo, 'Everyone according to his needs or everyone according to his deeds' (16/247), appears to be a misquotation (and perhaps a partial misunderstanding) of a pronouncement made by Karl Marx: 'From each according to his ability; to each according to his needs'. We feel that Bloom

ought to develop and rely on more direct ways of expressing
his own ideas.

'Eumaeus', like 'Telemachus', alerts us to such disjunctions
at the outset with its comment that Bloom behaves in
'orthodox Samaritan fashion' (16/3), the Samaritans being, in
reality, conspicuously unorthodox. A certain absurdity also
arises from the inclusion, in this expansively wordy episode,
of abbreviations for terms which would almost invariably
appear in full in any other text—'e. d. ed.' (16/17), meaning
'exhausted', for example, or 'circs' (16/97) for 'circumstances'.

A further type of local irony deployed extensively in
'Eumaeus' involves the literalisation of metaphor. While he
sceptically inspects a postcard, Bloom uses the commonplace
phrase 'the two sides [of an argument]' in a casual conver-
sational way (16/567); then in the next line, 'turned back the
other side of the card', thus literalising his own metaphorical
comment. (A reciprocal pattern also appears occasionally: we
hear an anecdote involving the firing of a gun, then a few
pages later Bloom urges Stephen to drink his coffee by saying
'Have a shot at it now' 16/807].) Stuart Gilbert cites another
case where a metaphor used in the text seems to be drawn
from a literal happening depicted earlier: '"Though they
didn't see eye to eye in everything", Mr Bloom reflects, "a
certain analogy there somehow was, as if both their minds
were travelling, so to speak, in the one train of
thought". . . . This transitory intimacy "in the one train of
thought" was humorously prefigured in Mr Bloom's journey
from Westland Row station. "Nice mixup. Then jump in first
class with third ticket. What am I following him for?"' (Gilbert
368). Bloom sagely advises Stephen 'I wouldn't personally
repose much trust in that boon companion of yours who
contributes the humorous element, Dr Mulligan, as a guide,
philosopher and friend if I were in your shoes. He knows
which side his bread is buttered on though in all probability
he never realised what it is to be without regular meals' (16/
279-83). As we listen (with Stephen) to Bloom's wise counsel
we can hardly overlook the fact that Stephen is actually

wearing Mulligan's shoes, as if he inhabits Bloom's metaphor before he even hears it, and we may also recall that Mulligan, far from discriminating about which side of his bread is buttered, usually butters both sides, a practice which clearly denoted his character, and invited negative moral judgments about him, when we first learnt of it (1/447). Yet these ironic details do not discredit Bloom's essentially sound advice about Mulligan; indeed, they may reinforce our sense of its astuteness. Bloom also shows sensible scepticism in his response to the questionable narratives produced in the episode by the seaman who calls himself Murphy, none of whose reports sounds altogether authentic. (We may recall that 'Murphy' appears as a name assumed for purposes of concealment and deception in the *Dubliners* story 'An Encounter'.) Murphy, like Stephen, reportedly wears borrowed attire: he remarks of a 'seadog' acquaintance, 'Them are his trousers I've on me' (16/655). In the next line Murphy's use of the terms 'shaving' and 'brushup' recalls Mulligan (and the allusions to Mulligan in the opening lines of 'Eumaeus'), so enhancing the implications of concealed identities and duplicity.

'Penelope' resembles both 'Telemachus' and 'Eumaeus' in its extensive use of local irony. The episode can be linked with 'Telemachus', in particular, in certain ways. These episodes constitute the beginning and end of the novel: we are led to contrast Stephen (central in the first episode) with Molly (central in the last), but also to contrast Mulligan (the plump naysayer who dominates 'Telemachus') with Molly (the plump yeasayer from 'Penelope'); and to note various imagistic associations (the green sea, evoking bile and death, mentioned in 'Telemachus'; the red sea, suggesting menstrual blood and potential fertility, mentioned in 'Penelope').

Just as 'Telemachus', initiating the novel, cannot contain allusions to previous material, so 'Penelope', ending it, cannot allude forward. But 'Penelope' also introduces us to a new sensibility, since it brings our first direct and extended contact with Molly's thoughts, and thus seems to break abruptly from the novel's earlier text as well. The style of 'Penelope' differs markedly from the styles of all the novel's other episodes, most obviously in its lack of any narrative intrusion into the stream of the central character's consciousness. Inter-episode allusions are also limited by Molly's exclusion from the action of the novel's earlier sections: she has appeared to us only briefly in 'Calypso', and momentarily in 'Wandering Rocks'. Molly, though she has a lively mind, is unintellectual and unreflective by comparison with Stephen and even with Bloom, and these qualities limit the opportunity for inter-textual and other allusions of the kind found in episodes like 'Proteus' or 'Lestrygonians'.

If the self-enclosure which correlates with local irony operates thematically in 'Telemachus' or 'Eumaeus', it does so as well in 'Penelope'. Here, the chief setting — the Blooms' bed — is still more restricting than the Martello tower or the cabman's shelter. As in 'Telemachus' or 'Eumaeus', some movement outside the chief setting occurs, but now the movement constitutes no more than Molly's visit to the chamber pot, an expedition which may be necessary and liberating but seems scarcely odyssean. As we read the text of 'Penelope' we feel confined to Molly's mind, even more rigorously than we were confined to Stephen's mind in 'Proteus', for example, or to Bloom's in 'Lestrygonians'. Molly likes to synthesise discrete entities whose disparities might make other people despair, or at least react with caution. She seems an appropriate Penelope figure in this further sense (besides being as faithful to her husband as can reasonably be expected). As Gordon notes, Molly is a person who 'grew up at the intersection of Atlantic and Mediterranean, Europe and Africa, north and south (Joyce romanticised the Spanish connections of Nora's native Galway), land, sea and sky . . . [and] whose entire reverie is consequently a search for re-convergence' (Gordon 124). Such patterns do mark the monologue, though we could also argue that Molly's search for 're-convergence' culminates in her acceptance of the impossibility of attaining it. We realise during the episode how Molly feels, with reason, that her life is limited and lonely. Bloom neglects her sexually and in other ways; Boylan is her first and only 'lover' in ten years, and there is in fact no pretence that he loves her or even that he strongly prefers her to other women; their affair, once detached from Molly's occasional euphoria and Bloom's moments of keenly felt anxiety, seems tawdry and cliché-ridden. Molly has few social contacts and even receives few letters. *Ulysses* has conveyed the sense, though it may do so chiefly by invoking Bloom's exaggerated worries, that most men in Dublin think Molly glamorous. In reality, as she now reminds us, her life is much more dreary than such an image allows.

Molly's mind nonetheless appears richer and more energetic in some ways than we might have expected it to be, and the limitations of setting and point of view work to emphasise these qualities by ironic contrast. Admittedly, some of the moral failings which critics have delighted in attributing to Molly would be difficult or impossible to disprove: she contradicts herself persistently, especially on the subject of men and their behaviour, and while some of these contradictions are merely flippant and amusing, others seem illogical, disruptive and potentially damaging. Molly also acknowledges various arbitrary and superstitious assumptions about reality, yet can be wilful and dogmatic on the subject of her own personal views. Although the novel's earlier critics often professed shock at Molly's supposedly frank observations about sex, they seemingly overlooked the fact that these remarks are largely private thoughts, most of which she would never express, even to Bloom or Boylan. Molly professes to feel some shock of her own about various sexual practices which most people — even in Dublin in 1904 — would probably consider commonplace, and while her sexual feelings have understandably been heightened by the day's encounter with Boylan, her attitudes to sexuality remain conventional enough. The 'richness' and 'energy' of her mind, rather, appear most strikingly in her sometimes lyrical recollections and evocations of her past life in Gibraltar, which she contrasts with her present existence in Dublin — mostly to the disadvantage of the present context; and occasionally in her thoughts about other people including, especially at the end of the episode, her husband. Molly clearly has powers of imagination which the novel's earlier episodes have not prepared us to expect. Memory is evoked and dramatised more fully in 'Penelope' than in earlier episodes. These discoveries by readers have, of course, their own ironic facets. Irony is also provided by the frequently conspicuous disjunction between Molly's bold declarations and conflicting facts in the external world (some of them known to us more fully than to Molly). She reflects of Stephen 'I suppose hed like my nice cream too' (18/1506). Having read 'Ithaca', we know that he has already had most of it, in response to Bloom's hospitable offer: Bloom 'served extraordinarily to his guest and, in reduced measure, to himself the viscous cream ordinarily reserved for the breakfast of his wife Marion (Molly)' (17/363-5). Molly also imagines that Bloom would like to have his toast 'buttered on both sides' (18/1244); but of course we know that this custom actually characterises Buck Mulligan.

Textual irony serves further to illuminate or emphasise particular aspects of Molly's thought processes. At the core of her thinking is a pattern of self-contradiction which parallels, and is aptly illustrated by, local ironies of the kind also deployed in 'Telemachus' and 'Eumaeus'. Molly comments that Bloom and other men insist on questioning women about their movements: 'were not to ask any questions but they want to know where were you where are you going' (18/299-300). But 'Ithaca' has already conveyed the implication that Molly undertakes such questioning more thoroughly than she undergoes it: we hear that Bloom's 'complete

corporal liberty of action had been circumscribed . . . by
various reiterated feminine interrogation concerning the mas-
culine destination whither, the place where, the time at
which, the duration for which, the object with which in the
case of temporary absences, projected or effected' (17/2291-7).
As James Van Dyck Card remarks, Molly 'deplores the way
her husband "plots and plans", even as her [own] mind is full
of schemes' (Card 40). Card also comments, 'we like to think
that we cannot have something both ways, but Joyce has
made certain that with Molly Bloom there is, in fact, more
than a possibility, for she is the deliberate embodiment of
contraries, which is to say, of Joyce's sense of them' (Card
42). Some of Molly's shifts of emphasis, though they may
concern only trivial or passingly relevant matters, are startlingly rapid; she thinks about a murderer, 'a big brute like
that that would attack a poor old woman to murder her in her
bed Id cut them off him so I would not that [Bloom would] be
much use still better than nothing' (18/997-9), and then
proceeds to depict Bloom's extreme incompetence at dealing
with prowlers.

Molly's self-contradictions, like the local ironies, tend to
operate bidirectionally: a later comment may qualify an
earlier one but, equally, an earlier comment may qualify a
later one. That these processes work in such a reciprocal or
spatial manner, as do the novel's local ironies, stresses
Molly's blithe capacity for noting only selective evidence and
ignoring whatever fails to suit her immediate concerns, for
forgetting at will a matter which had closely interested her
only moments earlier. Moreover, it aligns her monologue
with the structural patterns of *Ulysses* in a manner which the
apparent formlessness of her thoughts might otherwise seem
to undermine. Molly's self-contradictions also have, however, a more positive side; they admit the possibility of
affirmative, corrective re-evaluations, like understanding and
forgiveness: 'he [Bloom] used to be pretending to be laid up
with a sick voice doing his highness to make himself interesting for that old faggot Mrs Riordan . . . still I like that in him

polite to old women ... hes not proud out of nothing' (18/2-17).

Molly's monologue also incorporates several instances of unconsciously literalised metaphor which recall those prominent in 'Eumaeus'. Recollecting an early encounter with Mulvey, Molly reflects that 'it never entered my head what kissing meant till he put his tongue in my mouth' (18/770-71), the metaphorical penetration of her head immediately followed by a physical one. As in 'Eumaeus', the opposite process also occurs, as we see in Molly's presumably inadvertent allusion, made while she is sitting on the chamber pot, to the procedures of a parliamentary chamber: 'I better not make an alnight sitting on this affair they ought to make chambers a natural size' (18/1195-6). (Her phrase 'an alnight sitting on this affair' could also be seen as a broadly accurate description of the whole 'Penelope' episode, if we paraphrased it loosely as 'a lengthy, nocturnal, analytical meditation centrally concerned with a current extramarital involvement'.)

Local ironies appear in all the novel's episodes, and numerous other examples might have been cited to illustrate the points made here. The three episodes chosen for consideration, however, seem to deploy local ironies with particular insistence. In addition to those factors specific to each of the three episodes, already discussed, which help to explain this emphasis, we may locate factors common to all three which make a further contribution to the aptness of local irony, and which only become noticeable when the episodes are compared. Such elements may also mark all the novel's other episodes, in various measure, in proportion to their differing degrees of dependence on this mode of irony.

Each of the three episodes, 'Telemachus', 'Eumaeus' and 'Penelope', displays an ironic discrepancy between the episode's ostensible mood or tone and its actual deeper development. In 'Telemachus', which is a more subtle and complex episode than many of the elaborately experimental ones placed later in the novel, this process works with particular intricacy. The episode establishes a contrast between an elegant, formal style, expressing Mulligan's grandiloquent demeanour, and a confused and uncertain style, expressing Stephen's troubled state of mind. It is true that, as the episode suggests, these two characters oppose one another in many aspects of their lives; but both the styles are also misleading. We become more aware as we read episodes later in the novel that Mulligan's façade, as it appears to us in 'Telemachus', is flimsy. He remains ebullient and witty, but his hypocritical aspect, it becomes increasingly obvious, characterises him pervasively and distinctly; it is not a quality which Stephen glibly attributes to him without cause. Our probing of the surface of Mulligan's presentation in 'Telemachus', an operation which Joyce's persistent irony encourages us to undertake, alerts us precisely to these shades of interpretation. Equally, Stephen appears in later episodes as more substantial than he seems in 'Telemachus': more talented, less self-pitying. Again, Joyce challenges us, in the novel's opening episode, to ponder those qualities in Stephen which do not appear on the surface and which may even seem to be contradicted by his external demeanour. Local irony draws attention to such discrepancies. Thus the ostensible mood or tone of 'Telemachus', which springs largely from the antagonism between Stephen and Mulligan, has its own validity but also points to less apparent developments which we observe by noting the operation of the episode's local ironies.

'Eumaeus' shows similar discrepancies. Its tone seems talkative yet energetic, with words deployed expansively and extravagantly. Bloom and Stephen, however, appear tired, and tentative or diffident about initiating new action. As Schwarz remarks, 'within this most garrulous of chapters, the major communication between Bloom and Stephen is nonverbal and takes the form of looks and touches' (Schwarz 239). As in 'Telemachus', the disjunction between the episode's surface and its deeper implications alerts us to watch the details of character development and interaction closely.

In 'Penelope', we sense a discrepancy between Molly's often bold and assertive manner and much of the episode's content. Admittedly, our perception of her manner is confined, in literal terms, to her thought processes; hence it is less rigorously tested by contact with the external world than were the dominant tones of 'Telemachus' or 'Eumaeus'. Nonetheless, the same kind of disjunction, supported by numerous instances of local irony, appears in Molly's monologue. Particularly noticeable is the gap between Molly's emphatic and dogmatic pronouncements—she is not a person who encourages conflicting views or debate—and her most striking habit, her persistent self-contradiction.

Thus all three episodes are marked by an ironic disjunction between surface mood and deeper action. Moreover, in each case this 'deeper action' in itself involves irony. In 'Telemachus', Stephen displays his own ironic awareness of double meanings and discrepancies—a mode of perception which will be emphasised again in 'Nestor' and 'Proteus'. The action of 'Eumaeus' illustrates the apparently irreconcilable discrepancies between Stephen and Bloom; it also hints at the limitations of verbal communication, as in the quotation of the garbled newspaper report, and it attempts to communicate many of its implications by non-verbal means, seemingly a logical impossibility in a novel. And the content of Molly's monologue is marked by internal self-contradictions which are as emphatic as the discrepancy between that content and her manner of presenting it.

3
Single-Episode Ironies

Joyce's most specific and local ironies, considered in the previous chapter, help to keep his style both engaged and engaging. Such ironies, in other words, assure readers of Joyce's earnest attention to the contours of his subjects, and simultaneously demand from those readers keen attention not only to his material but to his manner of presenting it.

These ironies also serve to remind us how persistently Joyce works in ironic ways, thus alerting us to watch for analogous patterns operating on a larger scale. Many such patterns seem more elusive than the local instances, since they require us to juxtapose a particular component of the novel with a textual (or extra-textual) entity which may be found some distance away.

Most closely akin to the local ironies, at least in spatial terms, are those ironies which develop progressively throughout a particular episode. They demand that we perceive the episode in question much as we envisage a sentence or paragraph which is strongly marked by local irony. These 'intra-episode' ironies, like the local cases, serve at once to guide our manner of reading and to convey specific thematic material. Such ironies occur in all the episodes of *Ulysses*, but here it seems most useful to concentrate on two episodes which especially depend on them: 'Wandering Rocks' and 'Ithaca'.

'Wandering Rocks' could be called the 'most ironic' episode in the novel, for several reasons. It incorporates the widest variety of ironic modes, from the most specific to the most universal; in particular, it probably includes more numerous ironic links to the 'real world' than any other episode, and makes the most varied use of them. Moreover, the episode demands a constantly ironic mode of reading, in which we must acknowledge disjunctions and consider the alternative possibilities of meaning which lurk beneath all explicitly asserted ones. And, more pervasively than any other episode, it conveys the theme that the world of *Ulysses* is necessarily an ironic world: that apparently disparate or unrelated phenomena may be linked by ironic connections, and that apparently cognate, congruous or mutually sympathetic phenomena may be riven by ironic disjunctions.

Although in his construction of this episode Joyce adheres meticulously to temporal and spatial order, as Hart has carefully demonstrated (Hart and Hayman 181-216), the appearance of the flow of time and the fixity of objects in space does suffer frequent disturbances. In consequence, we need to read with particular attention, and we also gain a sense that our everyday assumptions about space and time may be alarmingly fragile.

The episode begins as Conmee 'reset his smooth watch in his interior pocket' (10/1-2). This phrase suggests Conmee's empathetic attachment (which may seem to us rather excessive in a priest) to a time-bound world. The watch is presumably 'smooth' because it has been consulted so frequently. The phrase also poses a momentary snare for the reader: to 'reset' a watch is usually to change the time it shows. Only the subsequent mention of Conmee's pocket indicates the true meaning: that he returns the watch to its customary place in his pocket. When Conmee consults his watch we do hear the time ('Five to three'), and Conmee's consequent reflection 'Just nice time to walk to Artane' seems to establish a precise, if leisurely, temporal and spatial structure for the episode. Later in 'Wandering Rocks', however, characters repeatedly consult watches or clocks to their own apparent enlightenment but to our simultaneous perplexity, since the time is not disclosed to us. We hear, for example, that Boylan 'drew a gold watch from his fob and held it at its chain's length' (10/312-13), but the result of his scrutiny of the watch remains unspecified. In the final section of the episode we are told that 'John Henry Menton, filling the doorway of Commercial Buildings, stared from winebig oyster eyes, holding a fat gold hunter watch not looked at in his fat left hand not feeling it' (10/1229-31); in this case, even the character seems to have become indifferent to questions of time, and we might reflect that his insensitivity to temporal textures parallels his insensitivity to other matters. We may hear that a clock is 'very large and wonderful and keeps famous time' (10/828), but such measures and such criteria often seem inadequate in this episode.

Conmee's sense of his own smooth and easy affinity with the temporal order is suddenly and amusingly undercut when he asks Mrs Sheehy how her sons are getting on at Belvedere (10/20-21) since, as Kenner and Robert Martin Adams have both pointed out, her sons had in fact left Belvedere some years before (Adams 14; Kenner 1980: 66). Conmee's mistake recounted at the beginning of 'Wandering Rocks', incidentally, recalls quite precisely Gabriel Conroy's mistake recounted at the beginning of 'The Dead', where he asks Lily (with whom he speaks on familiar and slightly condescending terms) about her current experiences at school, only to be informed that she has 'done schooling this year and more' (*D* 178). That Conmee may have been embarrassed in his encounter by Mrs Sheehy's observation of his absent-mindedness seems suggested by the briskness and earnestness of his conversation with three schoolboys immediately afterwards: 'Yes: they were from Belvedere. The little house. Aha. And were they good boys at school? O. That was very good now' (10/41-2). Mahaffey comments further that 'Joyce's relentless exposure of the easefully oblivious Conmee showcases a double irony: the irony of acting according to one's lights, a euphemism for acting ignorantly, and of using the unfocused notion of individual lights as a vague defense for one's own ignorance' (Mahaffey 119).

The 'interpolations' of material from one section of the

episode into another often function ironically. They seem designed to convey the thematic notion of temporal and spatial fragility: perceived relationships in space and time can be easily misconceived or upset. They also ensure our sustained attentiveness to all the characters, scenes and events depicted in the episode, rather than allowing us to focus only on one case at a time; and they suggest that the associations which might link apparently discrete people, settings or happenings together may need to be sought in unlikely places.

All the interpolations can be linked ironically to their thematic context. The first case, for example, introduces Mr Denis J. Maginni to us amid the account of Conmee's stroll; it is clearly an interpolation, since Maginni at the time is half a mile away from Conmee and invisible to him: 'Mr Denis J Maginni, professor of dancing &c, in silk hat, slate frockcoat with silk facings, white kerchief tie, tight lavender trousers, canary gloves and pointed patent boots, walking with grave deportment most respectfully took the curbstone as he passed lady Maxwell at the corner of Dignam's court' (10/56-60). This interpolation links itself tenuously to Conmee through its inclusion of the name 'Dignam', since Conmee's expedition is concerned with the Dignam family; much more significantly, the account of Maginni emphasises by reflection Conmee's own vanity and sycophancy. (Maginni dresses, we might notice, as colourfully as the foppish Mulligan; and, more immediately, he relishes contact with upper-class women, as Conmee does.)

The fourth section of the episode, set in the Dedalus household, contains three interpolations which all function ironically. Conmee appears in the first one:

—Did you put in the books? Boody asked.

Maggy at the range rammed down a greyish mass beneath bubbling suds twice with her potstick and wiped her brow.

—They wouldn't give anything on them, she said.

Father Conmee walked through Clongowes fields, his thinsocked ankles tickled by stubble.

—Where did you try? Boody asked.

—M'Guinness's.

Boody stamped her foot and threw her satchel on the table.

—Bad cess to her big face! she cried.

(10/260-69)

This interpolation, almost uniquely in the episode, presents a recollection of the past rather than an incident occurring simultaneously with the material in the surrounding section: Conmee is physically nowhere near Clongowes at the moment, nor at any other time in the episode. (This interpolation has, however, been anticipated by Conmee's own conscious recollection of his Clongowes days—a flashback rather than an interpolation—in the episode's first section.) This temporal disjunction throws emphasis onto the ironic and thematic (rather than structural) aspects of the interpolation. Mrs M'Guinness, the pawnbroker, has already appeared during the episode's first section in an encounter with Conmee. Conmee admires her 'carriage' (way of walking) but clearly feels that her present role as a pawnbroker is beneath his own dignity; yet at the time when he meets her, we now learn in the episode's fourth section, she has just refused to exchange the Dedalus girls' books for money which they urgently need to buy food. The shirts and peasoup boiling simultaneously on the Dedalus stove graphically demonstrate the family's poverty; and Boody's question to her sister, 'Did you put in the books?', might momentarily, surrealistically suggest that the books themselves have gone into one of the pots—to form that 'greyish mass' which is later identified as shirts. Moreover, Conmee's Clongowes period recalls Stephen's schooldays, which were depicted in the *Portrait*; this link seems especially appropriate here since the books Maggy has been trying to pawn include Stephen's books dating from that same era, as he reflects ruefully when he browses at the bookstall later in the episode: 'I might find here one of my pawned schoolprizes. *Stephano Dedalo, alumno optimo, palmam ferenti*' (10/840-41). A third connotation of this interpolation reinforces our awareness of Conmee's lack of charity, since Maggy's despairing declaration that she could make no money from the books is immediately followed by the mention of Conmee; the pawnbroker 'wouldn't give anything' on the books, and Conmee won't give anything to the one-legged sailor. (Incidentally, an ironic parallel might also be drawn between the attempt by the Dedalus girls to pawn Stephen's books, and the attempt by Bloom to rent a book for Molly.)

The second interpolation in this section simply involves the mention of the lacquey and the sound of his bell. The reference remains cryptic (if a little threatening) at the moment, but in the episode's eleventh section the lacquey's bell becomes a motif associated with the Dedalus family's poverty; thus the case in the fourth section becomes an ominous piece of foreshadowing. The plaintive sound of the lacquey's bell also contrasts with the 'joybells' imagined by Conmee (10/156). And the third interpolation reports the progress of the 'Elijah' throwaway down the Liffey. Here, as has been pointed out before, it is mentioned as a gloss on the theme of parent-child relationships. The Dedalus girls have conveyed some exasperation with their improvident father, notably in Boody's sardonic reference to 'Our father who art not in heaven' (10/291); and this mood interacts ironically with Elijah's Biblical role as reported in Malachi 4, 5-6: 'Behold, I will send you Elijah the prophet before the coming of the great and dreadful day of the Lord: And he shall turn the heart of the fathers to the children, and the heart of the children to their fathers, lest I come and smite the earth with a curse'.

Interpolations continue to function ironically throughout 'Wandering Rocks'. Two further examples appear in the eighth and ninth sections of the episode.

In the eighth section Parnell's brother, the chess-player and city marshal, makes a cryptic cameo appearance:

> In the still faint light he [Ned Lambert] moved about, tapping with his lath the piled seedbags and points of vantage on the floor.
> From a long face a beard and gaze hung on a chess-board.
> —I'm deeply obliged, Mr Lambert, the clergyman said. I won't trespass on your valuable time . . .   (10/423-7)

Here, the phrase 'points of vantage' suggests a game of chess. The chess-playing owner of the beard and gaze, however, remains for the moment unidentified. In the episode's fifteenth section Jimmy Henry complains of the marshal's absence from the council chamber; in the sixteenth section, John Howard Parnell finally appears in the flesh, as if translated from one section of text to another as he has been translated from the council chambers to the D. B. C., and engrossed in his game of chess, while Mulligan obligingly completes the pattern by identifying him as the missing marshal (10/1042-53).

In the ninth section Master Patrick Aloysius Dignam, who will reappear as the central figure in the eighteenth section, appears briefly with his 'pound and a half of porksteaks' (10/535), which are juxtaposed with Lenehan's mention of the 'long spread out at Glencree reformatory' (10/536). The social implications of this juxtaposition may be extended by the connection between Lenehan's gloss on the annual dinner, 'Boiled shirt affair' (10/537), and the shirts which we have already seen boiling on the stove in the Dedalus home (10/272). The meaning and the irony are also complicated, as Hart has noted, by the fact that young Dignam will go to an institution which closely resembles the reformatory (Hart and Hayman 208).

Money appears often in 'Wandering Rocks' as a particular sign of social relationships which have gone awry. Joyce encourages us to link the various financial references together through situational and imagistic echoes. Most obviously, he refers repeatedly to the same amount of money, five shillings, as central in numerous transactions. Five shillings, of course, constitute a 'crown', and the persistent allusions to this amount help subtly to convey the satiric connotations marking Joyce's treatment of the British crown and hence the British state, which appears in this episode as especially mercantile and materialistic. It seems particularly ironic that the first such 'crown' invoked should be in the possession of a priest, Father Conmee (10/11). Conmee appears to have taken this single large coin with him partly to avoid the necessity of giving money to beggars, something he refuses to do in the episode's second paragraph, even though he later uses the same crown to pay a penny tram fare. Thus the crown becomes for the moment an ironic symbol of possessiveness and of meanness; and through Conmee it links the state and the church, implying that both institutions are marked by such attributes.

References to money in general and to crowns in particular colour the entire episode. In one case Joyce invokes a specific contrast between Conmee's five shillings, which illustrate his reluctance to behave charitably, and Bloom's five shillings, which he does bestow in a charitable way on the Dignam family: we learn in the episode's fifteenth section that Bloom has 'put his name down for five shillings . . . and put down the five shillings too' (10/974-6). This contrast between Conmee and Bloom is further emphasised by the ostensible purpose of Conmee's expedition on which he ignores the sailor's plight: helping the Dignam family. In the episode's eleventh section, which is largely concerned with the poverty of the Dedalus family, we hear that the auctioneer expects to sell some curtains for five shillings (10/646-8). (The supposedly 'lovely curtains' [10/646] on sale here contrast with the more realistically described 'dingy curtain' [10/598] in the bookshop, another place characterised by financial transactions; we might compare the contrast between the joybells and the lacquey's bell.) Shortly afterwards, when Simon

Dedalus hands his daughter Dilly one shilling, she responds, 'I suppose you got five [shillings]' (10/680), again associating this particular amount of money with acts of charity, completed or otherwise. Simon thus gives a little money to his daughter, but he seems sparing and grudging by comparison with Bloom's generosity to the family of a virtual stranger (this comparison may be reinforced in the present scene through the similarity of the names of the two men's daughters: Milly, Dilly). More amusingly, Simon's response to Dilly's plea that he look for some money, 'I looked all along the gutter in O'Connell street. I'll try this one now' (10/703-4), is echoed less than forty lines later by Tom Kernan's reflection that 'where there's money going there's always someone to pick it up' (10/736-7), a gloss on corrupt practices. And Stephen appears still more parsimonious than his father, since he gives Dilly nothing at all when he meets her, even though he has the bulk of his month's salary in his pocket—money which he proceeds to spend mostly on drink.

The pattern of references to money becomes particularly complex, however, when Molly is involved. In the episode's third section, Molly (or at least her 'plump bare generous arm' [10/251]) appears tossing a coin to the same one-legged sailor who had vainly sought alms from Conmee in the first section. (We might notice, incidentally, that the sailor is missing a leg, while all we see of Molly in the course of this incident—in the course of the whole episode, indeed—is her arm. Joyce's use of the term 'alms' [10/9] may also conceal a pun.) Molly thus, inadvertently and ironically, associates herself and Bloom as bestowers of charity; and the link is reinforced specifically by her gesture of tossing down the coin from her window, since we are to hear that Bloom 'put down' the money for the Dignam family. Molly's gesture, while it seems generous, is nevertheless more ambivalent than it first appears; and it serves ironically to link the episode's financial concerns with other kinds of transaction and with other expressions of value.

Molly's throwing of the coin is depicted in a brief anticipatory interpolation within the episode's second section; there, her gesture appears ironically juxtaposed with Corny Kelleher's act of sending 'a silent jet of hayjuice arching from his mouth' (10/221). This juxtaposition makes Molly's act seem less pleasant than it might appear in isolation—especially since Kelleher is known to be a police informer. The 'stout lady' who gives the sailor a coin in the third section (10/238) also anticipates, without enhancing, Molly's act. This third section, indeed, abounds in parallels, as between the 'two barefoot urchins' (10/244) and the impoverished Katey and Boody Dedalus who are making their way home from school (10/233); the phrase *'home and beauty'* from the song (10/248) also seems to attach itself, with sad irony, to the two Dedalus girls. (That the girls are proceeding homewards slowly and reluctantly may be deduced from the ease with which the one-legged sailor, moving awkwardly along Eccles Street in the same direction, overtakes them.) Such an insistence on explicit parallels, especially marked in this particular section of the episode, encourages us to remain alert for other examples, some of which may be less conspicuous.

Crucially, the sailor's line *'For England, home and beauty'* comes from the song 'The Death of Nelson'. He is thus a one-legged sailor singing a song which concerns a one-armed sailor. Stephen has earlier referred to Nelson as a 'onehandled' sailor (7/1018). Stephen himself can also be ironically (if symbolically) associated with the awkward progress of the one-legged sailor: in 'Wandering Rocks' Haines remarks that 'Shakespeare is the happy huntingground of all minds that have lost their balance' (10/1061-2), to which observation Mulligan replies, alluding to Stephen, 'You should see him . . . when his body loses its balance' (10/1066). These two comments, by Haines and by Mulligan, flank an interpolation which alludes directly to the one-legged sailor, thus clearly linking him with Stephen, and which places the sailor currently in Nelson street, thus emphasising the connotations of the title of his song. Nelson stands in *Ulysses* for English imperialism (seen from an Irish political viewpoint) and, especially, for adultery: he is thus a figure who embodies several modes or levels of betrayal.

Molly sings as the sailor approaches; indeed, they perform simultaneously. Molly acknowledges this coincidence in 'Penelope', recalling the moment 'when I threw the penny to that lame sailor for England home and beauty when I was whistling there is a charming girl I love' (18/346-8). (The word 'lame', incidentally, seems a little inadequate as a label for the one-legged sailor's severe disability, especially given Bloom's praise for Molly's power to perceive afflictions of precisely the same kind: 'When I said to Molly the man at the corner of Cuffe street was goodlooking, thought she might like, twigged at once he had a false arm. Had, too' [13/914-16]. We might deduce that Molly has paid little close attention to the sailor's plight, presumably because she has been so preoccupied with Blazes Boylan's forthcoming visit.) Molly's 'duet' with the sailor anticipates the shared musical activities in which she and Boylan will engage soon afterwards. And the one-legged sailor, making his physically conspicuous way along Eccles Street, ironically anticipates the later, more decisive, and explicitly sexual aspect of Boylan's 'performance': we hear that the sailor 'swung himself forward in vigorous jerks' (10/246).

This scene of the giving of the coin, conspicuous because it constitutes Molly's only appearance to us between Bloom's departure from the house and his return to it, thus acts as an ironic gloss on Molly's main offstage act of the day. In that act she plays music with, and then (plump, bare and generous) gives her 'home and beauty' to, the betrayer and adulterer, Blazes Boylan.

Finally, 'Wandering Rocks' contains many other image-patterns which work to give the episode an ironic tone and structure. Several such patterns concern or illustrate the notion of temporal discontinuity or lack of completion: the failure of events to turn out as expected, or of people to reach their destinations. Joyce establishes a faint parallel between this uncertainty about the future and a corresponding uncertainty about the past: the origins of present situations, as well as their outcomes, often appear to be shrouded in doubt.

Conmee, on his way to help the Dignam family, catches a tram with ease, but Master Patrick Dignam himself misses one (10/1153). Young Dignam is probably relieved by this incident, however, since he feels no enthusiasm for returning to the house of mourning; his reluctance to go home ironically echoes that of the Dedalus girls and, indeed, that of Bloom himself. Dignam's apparent failure to catch a tram here may even have been deliberately engineered, by himself or by his family, to keep him away for a longer time. Almidano Artifoni trots in vain after his tram (10/363-6), and consequently has to walk home, a process which takes him the duration of the episode: 'Wandering Rocks' ends at the precise moment when Artifoni disappears into his house. Though Artifoni does reach his goal as we watch, we might reflect that most of the characters in the episode do not; we never see Conmee or the viceroy, for example, arrive at their destinations. Disjunction is also mimed by the perverse tendency of objects to move from their expected positions, to vanish, to fail to appear on schedule, or to be of uncertain origin. The 'slab where Wolfe Tone's statue was not' (10/378) is a case in point: the missing statue—a piece of stone which cannot be found in its expected place—might be likened to the wandering rocks themselves, and we may also recall Stephen's comments on the statue of Nelson. Moreover, Tom Kernan, wishing to see the viceregal cavalcade, reflects that he has 'just missed that by a hair' (10/797), an image which, in its manner of evoking a failure in fulfilment, suits events throughout the episode. Most of the reactions of the citizens to the cavalcade are highly ironic, since they appear to show, or can be described verbally as showing, a respect which the characters seldom feel in reality (Hart provides a detailed account of this ironic sequence Hart and Knuth 31]). The Mirus charity bazaar, the viceroy's ostensible goal, seems to occupy little of his thoughts, and is only mentioned for the first time a few lines before the end of the episode (10/1268-9).

'Wandering Rocks', then, mimes the forms of ironic disjunction—some comic, some tragic—marking Joyce's urban landscape. It suggests that the components of that landscape, animate and otherwise, can best be understood through a process of comparison which pays adequate attention to patterns of congruity and of difference. Irony is Joyce's central method of conveying such perceptions.

'Wandering Rocks' and 'Ithaca' resemble one another in several respects, and can be usefully considered together as episodes where irony operates in particularly insistent and structurally determining ways. Both episodes appear to be written in an objective, scientific manner which ostensibly distances the narrative position from the characters and the characters from the reader. Karen Lawrence remarks that 'both the coldness and the mechanical cataloguing in "Ithaca" are anticipated in "Wandering Rocks"' (Lawrence 181). Normal assumptions about omniscient narrative are radically undercut in both episodes. Hart claims that in 'Wandering Rocks' there is a narrator who 'pretends to be innocent of self-knowledge' (Hart and Hayman 189). Lawrence adds that in the repeated references to 'a onelegged sailor', 'the narrative inability to progress from the indefinite to the definite article illustrates a strange failing in the "narrative memory"' (Lawrence 84); and that 'Ithaca' has a narrator who 'plows through a mass of facts laboriously, as if a name were a labor-saving device of which he had never heard' (Lawrence 187).

The two episodes are linked in their extreme exemplification of Joyce's distaste for exposition; both parody the very notion of scene-setting and undercut any aim to provide information about 'backgrounds', suggesting that such information, should we possess it, would only provide superficial and inadequate explanations. Both episodes leave gaps for us to fill as they present discontinuities, uncertain origins and outcomes, and ironic disjunctions.

'Ithaca' repeatedly, and still more insistently than 'Wandering Rocks', mimes a disjunctiveness, a fragmentation, for which the sheer continuity of the writing nevertheless implicitly proposes a kind of cure. Analysed dispassionately or assessed through a study of its smallest components, the episode (like 'Wandering Rocks') would often seem negative; yet in practice a reader will more probably feel a positive response to the text. This response suggests that readers react to the episode's ironies by trying to establish connections, rather than by accepting that the process of disintegration (which also appears as a conspicuous possibility) is inevitable. If 'Wandering Rocks' deploys irony in more varied ways than any other episode, 'Ithaca' takes the ironic manner to a different extreme, defined by depth and by remarkable stylistic poise.

Seasoned readers of *Ulysses* may easily underestimate or forget the sheer strangeness of Joyce's question-and-answer style in 'Ithaca'. Yet only repeated attention to the text of the episode (aided, perhaps, by the critical accounts which have been written about it) can make the manner seem familiar and accessible. The process by which such a bizarre narrative mode becomes available to readers is itself part of the meaning of the episode.

It is nevertheless difficult to imagine that the opening episode of any novel could be written in such a style. In reading 'Ithaca', we depend heavily on knowledge which we have derived from earlier episodes of *Ulysses*. The style of 'Ithaca' seems to suit the reworking of material supplied previously in the novel rather than the provision of new information (especially information related to plot and character). Although we learn numerous facts in this episode, they seem to modify only slightly the impressions which we have already formed. Answers are supplied, but some prior knowledge seems necessary in order for appropriate questions to be asked. However, some of the new information is more significant than it initially seems—for example, data which concerns Bloom's financial situation or Molly's affair with Boylan. As Kenner says, 'like the final chapter of a Victorian novel, "Ithaca" abounds in detailed revelations that refocus what we had thought we knew and substantiate what we only guessed' (Kenner 1980: 141).

'Ithaca' begins by asserting that phenomena are measurable and implying that they tend to the normative. In the episode's opening lines, emphasis falls heavily on such systematic words and phrases as 'parallel', 'united', 'normal', 'order', 'similarity', 'like and unlike', 'equal and negative'. A precise factual grid thus appears to be established at the outset, akin to the one we found suggested in the opening lines of 'Wandering Rocks'. Throughout the 'Ithaca' episode, the narrative tone remains calm and seemingly objective; everything appears remarkably and even startlingly 'normal', especially after the grotesque excesses of 'Circe' and the languid oddities of 'Eumaeus'.

Yet Joyce still seems concerned to question notions of the world as a precisely ordered, structured, measurable place. 'Ithaca' contains numerous factual errors which insidiously undermine any belief in the attainment of perfect form and order.

Some of these factual errors clearly reflect Joyce's deliberate policy, while others are of more dubious origin. A few examples seemingly derive from Joyce's involuntary arithmetical errors, while others were probably contributed to the novel by various people during the tortuous process of textual transmission. Such a blend of variety and uncertainty seems, in itself, appropriate. For all Joyce's well-known fastidiousness it is possible to imagine, in the context of details of measurement in 'Ithaca', that he might have tolerated or even welcomed occasional errors produced by outside agencies. Such a view of Joyce's motives may have been partially shared by Hans Walter Gabler as he worked on the 'corrected' text of *Ulysses*, though it seems to pose almost impossible difficulties of editorial procedure; at all events, Gabler has emended the text in a few cases where he believes

Joyce's mathematics were faulty, as well as in some less controversial cases which apparently derived from accidents in textual transmission. In a letter of 6 December 1921 to Harriet Weaver, Joyce remarks that 'as regards "Ithaca" the question of printer's errors is not the chief point. The episode should be read by some person who is a physicist, mathematician and astronomer and a number of other things' (*L I* 178). This declaration, though cryptic, does suggest that Joyce wished his mathematical and other ventures to be checked for errors by experts before the episode appeared in print.

In the list of anagrams which Bloom has composed from his own name (17/405-9), two of the examples have letters missing, and Joyce could scarcely have allowed them to appear in this way by accident. While the anagrams seem an agreeably impressionistic summary and anticipation of Bloom's actual or imagined life, the omission of the letters may hint that such mutations of his identity cannot occur without distortion or loss; we might also recall the injury suffered by his name in the newspaper account cited in 'Eumaeus'. Bloom's budget (17/1456-78), as many readers have noticed, appears remarkably precise—few people could record their expenses in such fastidious detail—yet is seemingly marred by a serious error of omission: the money Bloom spent in the brothel does not figure in the list. It is usually argued by critics that the budget omits transactions which Bloom would wish to conceal from Molly, though she might enquire about the postal order which Bloom bought for Martha and which does appear in the budget. It is also conceivable, though less likely, that the financial transaction in the brothel, like many other events in 'Circe', is of questionable authenticity and thus inappropriate for the budget's modes of measurement. In any case, the budget casts considerable doubt on the very notion of precise calculation and record.

The elaborate calculations based on the ratio of Bloom's and Stephen's ages (17/447-61) also fall into error. The eagerness of critics to draw attention to such mistakes, and even to deduce precisely how Joyce may have been led into them, threatens to disguise the remarkable pointlessness of the calculations—a wilful pointlessness which supports the view that Joyce intended these particular errors to appear in the text. In the case of one comparison with Stephen's age, it is hard to see what possible difference it can make whether Bloom 'would have been obliged to have been alive 83,300 years' (17/460) or, as several critics have solemnly informed us, only 20,230 years; Joyce would surely have been much amused by the critical debate on this point. (There is a marvellous redundancy in Richard M. Kain's mention of Stephen's and Bloom's 'impossible [sic] longevities of 374, 646, and finally 83,300 years' [Kain 154].)

Some of Bloom's physical measurements as supplied in 'Ithaca' seem implausibly small for a person of his build as it is specified elsewhere in the novel, a point noted by several critics (17/1815-19). It is conceivable that Joyce erred here. Other, more banal explanations than those offered to date may also be possible—as that Bloom had used the exercise machine (supposedly responsible for making his slender contours slightly less slender) in adolescence, rather than recently. Explanations advanced by a few critics, which postulate or require a surreal Bloom, are highly suspect. Adams remarks rather absurdly that Bloom 'might as plausibly have been assigned a head four inches in diameter—or four feet' (Adams 184). Jean Kimball adds that the implausible Bloom denoted by the measurements suits a man whose previous addresses include no house numbers (Kimball 203). But we hear of these addresses within Bloom's or Molly's interior monologue, and few people consciously include house numbers in their purely verbal recollections of previous addresses: most such thoughts take the form of Bloom's characteristic recall of the time when 'we were on the rocks in Holles street' (13/840-41) or of the moment when 'the painters were in Lombard street west' (13/1000-01). There is no need in such a context for us to recall house numbers unless we have had two addresses on the same street, which the Blooms have not done. Bloom's measurements may be odd, but the fault is in the figures, not in Bloom.

Further reflection on 'Ithaca' may lead us to characterise the episode's tone not as 'parallel' and 'normal' but by other phrases offered to us within its text—perhaps 'alternately stimulating and obtunding' (17/25). Joyce's reference to 'the false apparent parallelism of all perpendicular arms of all balances' (17/690) also seems a wry gloss on the flawed factual grid of the episode, as do the traumatic rearrangement of Bloom's furniture and Bloom's consequent collision with his sideboard. 'Ithaca' seeks to demonstrate the limitations and inadequacies of mere information. Any phenomenon can be detailed and defined, but it may not thereby be fixed or explained. Truth, we are supposed to reflect, may reside in those portions of a problem which are particularly difficult to measure, or which cannot readily be produced as answers to specific questions. Lawrence remarks of the episode: 'Ironically, no answer is definitive because it has the potential to generate another, more specific question, which leads to another answer, and so on' (Lawrence 190). MacCabe adds that '"Ithaca", in its surplus of answers, provides no place for the reader from which the text will make sense' (MacCabe 131).

The gap between question and answer, indeed, becomes a recurrent preoccupation in 'Ithaca'. The episode's structure repeatedly raises the expectation that any question can be answered, then proceeds to undermine that expectation. Answers may ostensibly respond in an honest way to their particular questions, yet still supply either insufficient or excessive detail (two responses which can be oddly similar in their effects) or data displaced in some other respect from the response which we might have anticipated. Well-known examples include the floods of information about the Dublin water-supply system, and about the properties in water which Bloom admires or might admire, which pour into the text at the slightest provocation—a stray Bloomian thought, the turning of a kitchen tap. Elliott B. Gose suggests in his essay, 'The Coincidence of Contraries as Theme and Technique in *Ulysses'*, that 'the questions of "Ithaca" . . . call forth the answers, but the answers often contend with the question, as when a pretentious question receives only a monosyllabic answer' (Newman and Thornton 215). Such gulfs between question and answer readily become ironic. The expectation that questions are always answerable may have analogies with a belief that non-ironic communication is possible — another belief challenged repeatedly by 'Ithaca'.

Joyce also uses his irony in 'Ithaca' to corroborate and qualify the implications of Stephen's meeting with Bloom. Irony ensures that dual or multiple possibilities of interpretation will jostle in the text: that the meeting cannot be seen simply as a success or a failure. The local and broader implications of the meeting differ from each other in kind and in the degree of their positive import; and they interact with each other as do the immediate and derived connotations of a given instance of literary irony.

Stephen and Bloom, the 'keyless couple' (17/81), themselves seem both united and separated, by the connotations of their personal characteristics, in a manner which we could well describe as ironic. An apparent affinity may mask a deeper divergence, or an apparent divergence may mask a deeper affinity. The gaps between Stephen and Bloom, in age, race, education, experience and personality, may appear crucial, or immaterial, in particular contexts which replace one another at bewildering speed.

Among Bloom's many proposals for the future is a series of meetings with Stephen: he wishes 'to inaugurate a series of static, semistatic and peripatetic intellectual dialogues, places the residence of both speakers (if both speakers were resident in the same place), the Ship hotel and tavern, 6 Lower Abbey street (W. and E. Connery, proprietors), the National Library of Ireland, 10 Kildare street, the National Maternity Hospital, 29, 30 and 31 Holles street . . . ' (17/964-9). This list seems neither plausible nor promising, but it does recapitulate, approximately, the series of places where Stephen has met or intended to meet Mulligan in the course of the day. The oblique implication, then, may be that Bloom could displace Mulligan as a companion for Stephen. But this conclusion remains unstated, and is conveyed by ironic adjustments in our view of the characters, rather than by developments in the plot.

'Ithaca' thus withholds the kind of plot resolution which many novels seek to provide. The episode, rather, draws energy from realignments of judgment akin to those demanded by irony: a configuration which initially appears logical or self-sufficient comes to require reappraisal, and so revalues its context. By the end of 'Ithaca' little has happened, but our view of the characters and their situation has been considerably refined.

Finally, then, Joyce plays in 'Ithaca' with ironic disjunctions between 'story' and 'discourse', between matter and manner. Schwarz asks: 'Is it too much to say that while the discourse or metaphorical level affirms Stephen's acceptance of Bloom as the necessary father figure and implies his future maturation, the story does not substantiate this?' (Schwarz 231). Such disjunctions mark the whole episode. Joyce also separates discourse from story through his arcane vocabulary—for example, in a sentence alluding to dogs, he uses the esoteric term 'latration' instead of its familiar synonym 'barking' (17/1951). Thus he challenges any easy positivist notions of the identity of signifier and signified. There is always a potential ironic divergence separating these components, Joyce would have us believe, a divergence which ensures that no meaning can ever be fixed with absolute precision. 'Ithaca' is designed not to overlook or blur such divergences, but to highlight them. It thus imposes on readers a kind of retrospective scepticism, both linguistic and epistemological, about their recollections of all the novel's previous episodes. It also wryly prepares us for the novel's one remaining episode, in which the apparent gap between meaning and language narrows and sometimes threatens to disappear altogether: 'Penelope'.

4
Inter-Episode Ironies

Many of Joyce's ironies in *Ulysses* link widely separated episodes: that is, the contexts required for revaluation of a particular ironic passage are to be found outside the episode containing it, but still within the text of the novel. Joyce often uses such inter-episode ironies as a structural device. *Ulysses* is tied together by various kinds of links associating widely separated segments of the text; ironies are a favourite kind of structural bond, perhaps partly because of the ways in which they energise their contexts in the novel, making both ends of the link operate as vital participants in the transaction.

Such ironies also have numerous semantic and thematic consequences. Joyce uses them to convey the implication that some situations—in literature and in life—cannot intrinsically provide adequate standards which might allow us to judge them, so that we will need to seek such values elsewhere. Moreover, apparent meanings and those which we are able to reconstruct, though widely spaced geographically in the text, can still join neatly if we notice the links that associate them; and life may also require us to make associations in such ways. Examples of this kind also emphasise the fact that ironies can work reciprocally: as we respond to them, we revalue the immediate context in which the corrective or 'true' meaning resides as well as the immediate context of the ironic marker or 'false' meaning which sent us in quest of truth in the first place. These in turn should be reassuring conclusions, both within the novel and in a wider context, implying among other things that no event which occurs is ever lost.

It would, no doubt, be possible to demonstrate ironic links between any given episode in *Ulysses* and any other episode. The exercise would become mechanical, and some of the connections might be tenuous, though Joyce worked at such patterns with great persistence. The present chapter, however, will focus on one particularly striking example linking 'Hades' and 'Penelope', then turn to consider the ironic associations between 'Nausicaa' and those episodes which display especially strong structural and thematic bonds with it.

Molly Bloom's liaison with Blazes Boylan, which follows a decade of sexual neglect, cheers her up for the moment, as she reflects movingly at the end of the novel in the 'Penelope' episode: 'O thanks be to the great God I got somebody to give me what I badly wanted to put some heart up into me youve no chances at all in this place like you used long ago' (18/732-4). Yet despite that brief moment of euphoria Molly does not expect her affair with Boylan to last, and she ends her monologue, and the novel, by recalling with some passion her life with her husband Leopold Bloom, who for all his faults has more 'spunk' and more life in him than Boylan does. The relationship with Boylan is, in itself, a dead end, and Bloom's qualities of compassion and imagination will eventually carry the day.

At the time he wrote Molly's monologue, Joyce was also revising the graveyard episode 'Hades', near the beginning of the novel, and some of the additions he made to that episode at this stage are clearly meant to serve as an anticipatory ironic gloss on 'Penelope' (or a retrospective one if we are re-reading). He incorporated several verbal and imagistic echoes which precisely link together Molly's recollections of her sexual encounter with Boylan, and Bloom's meditations on death given in the graveyard scene. These links collectively reinforce the notion that Boylan is a deathly presence. There are two particularly noticeable echoes. Molly recalls Boylan's crassness in undressing, uninvited, before her, and 'standing out that vulgar way in the half of a shirt they [men] wear to be admired' (18/1373-4). In Bloom's meditation on death he had imagined a depiction of the Devil showing a woman to a sinner, who responds by 'dying to embrace her in his shirt'

(6/852). Still more strikingly, Molly recalls that during Boylan's visit her marital bed, unaccustomed as it had become to having such strenuous exertions performed on it, had 'jingled' perturbingly, 'till I suggested to put the quilt on the floor with the pillow under my bottom' (18/1132-3), and she and Boylan evidently finish their encounter on a pillow on the floor. When he was imagining a man dying in a room in the 'Hades' episode, Bloom had reflected, 'Pull the pillow away and finish it off on the floor since he's doomed' (6/850-51).

This association is emphatic and precise, even though the relevant portions of the novel are found hundreds of pages apart. Once noticed, the association links and energises a number of apparently disparate contexts. Besides its most obvious function of reinforcing the association between Boylan and death, it also, through a further irony, links Bloom with Molly. Bloom's sensitivity, as revealed in the scenes he envisages in 'Hades', marks his superiority to the cardboard (or imaginatively dead) figure of Boylan, and helps explain Molly's impulse to return to him.

The 'Nausicaa' episode seems particularly dependent on such ironic associations with other episodes. There are several apt reasons for this dependence, and several apt consequences follow once the ironic evaluations are made.

Most obviously, 'Nausicaa' concerns itself with the realm of escapism and fantasy, with provisional attempts to evade external standards of judgment; it therefore seems appropriate (but also ironic) that the episode should at first appear self-enclosed, then progressively reveal unsuspected points of contact with other parts of the novel. Bloom, at this stage of his day, is static, tired, lonely and frustrated, depressed after the hostility he has encountered at Barney Kiernan's and the drab minutiae he has had to deal with at the Dignam household, reluctant also to return home and confront the reality of Molly's infidelity. Escape into reveries seems an obvious temptation for him, and such an escape is made all the more inviting by the apparently romantic setting (a beach at sunset, with a fireworks display and a church service in the background to provide local colour).

Moreover, the episode's other central character, Gerty MacDowell, has her own reasons for seeking an escape into fantasy: her largely repressed anxieties and frustrations caused by her lameness, her envy of her friends, and her family circumstances. Since Gerty has scarcely appeared in *Ulysses* before, apart from her brief cameo appearance in 'Wandering Rocks', she seems fresh and intriguing to us as well as to Bloom. Both characters yield to escapist temptations, with results which are inconclusive but not quite negligible: in the simultaneous self-induced orgasms of Bloom and Gerty, some communication and some consolation survive the silliness and the clichés which are also unmistakably present in the scene.

Yet to evaluate fully and precisely the events of this episode, we must notice the ironic connections with other episodes which Joyce carefully provides. Many of these connections add more dignity to the encounter between Bloom and Gerty than it would display in isolation. Such associations also show further dimensions of self-indulgence and self-deception in characters and events depicted elsewhere in the novel as we are led to juxtapose them with those appearing in 'Nausicaa'. The relationship between 'Nausicaa' and the rest of the novel thus undergoes a quiet inversion, in which the tone of 'Nausicaa' becomes more emphatically normative than it first appears, and we begin to see new signs of escapism in many other places. The episode with the most comprehensive pattern of ironic links to 'Nausicaa' is 'Proteus', which will be discussed later in this chapter. 'Nausicaa' also has precise ironic links to at least half the novel's other episodes, however, and the most important of these connections will be considered now.

A few such cases are specific and limited, but still change our sense both of 'Nausicaa' and of the other episode involved in the association. For example, the altercation between the two young boys over the possession of the 'tower' (sandcastle) on the beach in 'Nausicaa' recalls the symbolic struggle between Stephen and Mulligan, in 'Telemachus', over their rights to the Martello tower and the key to its door—especially since the boys quarrel with particular insistence over the proposal one of them has made that their castle would be 'architecturally improved by a frontdoor like the Martello tower had' (13/44-5). A childish dimension to the Stephen/Mulligan conflict is emphasised by this association, but we may also take the children's struggles more seriously in the light of the comparison with 'Telemachus', since they appear so precisely to anticipate adult battles.

Similarly, the child whose toilet formalities seem to threaten his smart 'new tan shoes' (13/77) might recall for us that Boylan was also displaying his 'new tan shoes' in 'Wandering Rocks' (10/307). The phrasing here is precise enough to link the two characters and the two scenes, so implying or reinforcing our impressions of Boylan's childishness and vanity, but also requiring us to take the children's experiences more seriously than do their guardians, one of whom professes a facile faith in 'the art of smoothing over life's tiny troubles' (13/57-8). The verbal link involving the shoes suggests that the boy could become a Boylan (the first syllable of whose surname seems especially resonant in this context), and although Bloom will wisely decide later that adultery is less serious than 'a cataclysmic annihilation of the planet in consequence of a collision with a dark sun' (17/2181-2), nevertheless 'the art of smoothing over life's tiny troubles' scarcely suffices to wish away something as decisive as a completed act of infidelity.

'Nausicaa' can also be associated with 'Wandering Rocks' through Gerty's appearance in that episode. In 'Wandering Rocks' Gerty, like other characters, appears hemmed in and frustrated by the grinding civic machinery of Dublin as well as by personal circumstances. She is seen 'carrying the Catesby's cork lino letters for her father who was laid up'; as the cavalcade passes, she 'knew by the style it was the lord and lady lieutenant but she couldn't see what Her Excellency had on because the tram and Spring's big yellow furniture van had to stop in front of her on account of its being the lord lieutenant' (10/1207-11). Here, as in 'Nausicaa' itself, Gerty seems associated with a conflict between a reality she sees as dreary, and the possibility of escaping in fantasy to something grander; Senn speaks of her experience as 'a frustrated vision into which reality crudely interferes' (Hart and Hayman 291), and even suggests, provocatively, that the rhythm of the sentence which describes Gerty walking in 'Wandering Rocks' evokes her limp, about which we have not yet been told. In any case, Gerty's appearance in 'Wandering Rocks' helps to prepare us for her pursuit of fantasies and palliatives in 'Nausicaa', while 'Nausicaa' retrospectively reinforces the pathos of 'Wandering Rocks' by reminding us, through Gerty's example, of the extreme measures which some of the other characters may need to take in order to escape from their miserable circumstances.

Gerty's brief preliminary appearance in 'Wandering Rocks' is balanced by her subsequent, more naturalistically problematic but also more revealing, appearance in 'Circe' (15/372-86). Here, her limp marks her movements at the outset, and the tone of the text throughout her time onstage bespeaks disillusionment and a harsh assault on romantic sentiment. We are now required to take Gerty more seriously than we may have done as we read 'Nausicaa', but also to reflect on the ambivalence of her situation and on the extent of her active participation in (and enthusiasm for) the 'Nausicaa' encounter. When she appears in 'Circe', Gerty is *'leering'* and *'ogling'* (15/372-3), as if to remind us that she can stare as well as being stared at. Recalling Bloom's actions in 'Nausicaa', she tells him 'I love you for doing that to me' (15/385). Bloom, by contrast, now absurdly (and ironically) seeks to deny the emphatically voyeuristic nature of their earlier encounter: 'I never saw you' (15/378).

Another specific association, this time involving the language of 'Nausicaa' rather than events depicted within it, ties the episode to the newspaper scene, 'Aeolus'. Both episodes are marked by linguistic excesses, which come to seem surprisingly similar when we compare them, even though the inhabitants of each of the verbal worlds in question would normally have nothing to do with those of the other. In other words, the frequently pompous 'male' rhetoric of politics, current events and newspaper reporting, dominant in 'Aeolus', may be no more adequate as a transcription of reality than the seemingly sentimental 'female' rhetoric of fashion, self-image and girls' magazines, featured in 'Nausicaa'. 'Nausicaa' thus casts a retrospective query over any temptation we may have felt to take the excesses of 'Aeolus' too seriously, while our earlier reading of 'Aeolus' should make the rhetoric explored in 'Nausicaa' seem more substantial than it would appear in isolation.

'Nausicaa' is also linked to the episodes which immediately precede and follow it; many of these links depend on irony. A structural link with its predecessor 'Cyclops' is wryly evoked by the imagery of rising and falling used at the end of 'Cyclops' and (on the novel's next few pages) at the beginning of 'Nausicaa'. At the end of the earlier episode we are invited to imagine Bloom 'ascend to the glory of the brightness at an angle of fortyfive degrees' (12/1916-17), as if he were one of the firework rockets frequently invoked in 'Nausicaa'. These rockets in turn will be ironically (and phallicly) linked with the sexual excitement which underlies the first half of 'Nausicaa'. Bloom's inevitable fall after his glorious rise at the end of 'Cyclops' seems to us to deposit him on the beach at the beginning of 'Nausicaa' (even though, in terms of his own life and of the novel's plot, he has in fact travelled to the Dignam house, and occupied himself for several hours, in the meantime). The firework rockets also inevitably fall darkly after their spectacular ascent, and this movement parallels the detumescent sadness marking the second half of 'Nausicaa', a mood further emphasised by Bloom's act of discarding the stick with which he had written inconclusively in the sand: 'He flung his wooden pen away. The stick fell in silted sand, stuck' (13/1270).

The association between 'Nausicaa' and 'Cyclops' is thematic as well as structural. It recalls the association between 'Nausicaa' and 'Aeolus' in some respects: a male rhetoric or discourse is juxtaposed with a female one, for example. In the case of the link between 'Nausicaa' and 'Cyclops', the comparison extends into other forms of behaviour besides modes of speech. 'Cyclops' parodies various extreme and negative forms of characteristically 'male' behaviour through its depiction of aggression, intimidation, violence, prejudice and xenophobia; while 'Nausicaa' similarly parodies negative 'female' forms in its attention to excessive sentiment, romantic self-delusion, lushness, vagueness and euphemism. Yet the act of juxtaposing the two episodes, as we will inevitably do because of their sheer geographical proximity in the novel, helps us to see that these apparently opposed modes of speech and action have more in common than we might have supposed. As Senn remarks in his judicious account of 'Nausicaa', 'the pathetic climax of the two chance lovers resembles Bloom's confrontation with the citizen [in "Cyclops"], an earlier blend of conviction, tumescent courage, irritation, and pulpit sentimentality' (Hart and Hayman 281). Both modes in question are extreme divergences from common middle ground, and both in their various ways obliquely suggest means by which that ground might be retrieved—through the avoidance of narrow-minded or one-eyed views of the world, for example. Particularly distorted in both episodes is the notion of love, which (for all Joyce's reticence on the subject) subsists as a central concern in *Ulysses*. A truer notion of love than those commonly considered in everyday life suggests itself as a crucial requirement, if the divisions between male and female views enacted in the contrast between 'Cyclops' and 'Nausicaa' are to be overcome. Such a notion will also be vital, of course, to the resolution of the plot of *Ulysses*, and so Joyce's exploration of aberrations of love in 'Cyclops' and in 'Nausicaa' constitutes an important moment in his narrative. Ironic disjunctions between the two episodes help to guide us in our assessment of these concerns.

Similarly, links between 'Nausicaa' and the episode which immediately follows it, 'Oxen of the Sun', are drawn to our notice by structural devices but also resonate thematically. The most obvious structural association appears in the triple repetition of threefold ritual sounds or chants both at the end of 'Nausicaa' and at the beginning of 'Oxen'; and the link between these two sets of sounds or chants seems precisely ironical since those in 'Oxen' concern themselves with child-birth and those in 'Nausicaa' with Bloom's cuckoldry. Less specific situational parallels are provided by Bloom's dis-placed and solitary position in both episodes, as other people chatter nearby (a configuration which is not, of course, confined to these two episodes alone, but which appears more strongly in them than it does elsewhere). Thematically, 'Nausicaa' and 'Oxen' are associated through Joyce's explora-tion in both episodes of sexual roles, especially those assumed by women, and the attitudes adopted towards such roles by members of the other sex. Irony, again, works in both directions here. The callowness of the male medical students in 'Oxen' undercuts the fantasy projections of the girls in 'Nausicaa' about topics like marriage and childbirth; but the wiliness of Gerty's friends also casts doubt on the facile sexist assumptions made by Mulligan and his associ-ates. This link seems a more social and urbane version of the sexual disjunction mimed by 'Cyclops' and 'Nausicaa'; it is as though the values evoked in 'Nausicaa' are assailed in the text from both sides. Limited male values reappear in 'Oxen', as if to remind us that the assertion of female priorities in 'Nausicaa' may not suffice to banish the male values perma-nently.

Apart from 'Proteus', four other episodes not so far con-sidered here have vital associations with 'Nausicaa': 'Ithaca', 'Penelope', 'Sirens' and 'Lotus Eaters'.

We may link 'Nausicaa' with 'Ithaca' since both episodes include extended meditations by Bloom; and he falls asleep at the end of each of these meditations, in an ambivalent act which illustrates his exhaustion but also conveys a sense of completion and even achievement. Moreover, 'Nausicaa' should already have shown us that Gerty MacDowell and Bloom have more in common than initially meets the eye, especially in their shared impulse to take refuge in fantasy. 'Ithaca' reinforces our awareness of this affinity. Bloom's vision of domestic bliss, announced fulsomely in 'Ithaca', disquietingly resembles Gerty's; and our previous exposure to Gerty's views in 'Nausicaa' ironically casts an anticipatory doubt on the value of Bloom's aspirations. As with so many inter-episode ironies, however, this case operates in the opposite direction as well. If Bloom (whom we have grown to admire) can manage no loftier a conception of household contentment than the one we see him entertain in 'Ithaca', then the deficiency, the difficulty of attaining such a vision, may be located in the world outside rather than in Bloom. If so, then surely Gerty (who has far less experience of life than Bloom has) cannot be justly faulted for her inability to envisage any grander notion of home comforts than the one she reveals in 'Nausicaa'.

Striking affinities also link 'Nausicaa' and 'Penelope'. Some connections of this kind might seem inevitable, since these are the novel's most completely 'female' episodes, but Joyce elaborates the connections well beyond such structural necessities. Gerty, a substitute for Molly in Bloom's erotic imagination, in many respects prepares us for our own encounter with Molly, whom we have met earlier in the novel but who remains a largely enigmatic presence until we overhear her thoughts in 'Penelope'. Gerty and Molly share a number of mannerisms, habits and preoccupations, embodied most generally in their flowing interior monologues. Both characters make extensive use of the word 'because', a word which Joyce facetiously characterised as feminine, implying that women use it not to herald a logical explanation of cause but rather to camouflage the absence or failure of such explanations. Both characters can be superstitious, show an interest in fashion, and make shrewd judgments, especially about other women. Gerty is considerably younger than Molly, but precisely for that reason recalls for Bloom his early days with her; she is seemingly beginning (like Molly in 'Penelope') to menstruate; and she appears to Bloom receptive, attractive and arousing. Thus Gerty can be seen not as the occasion for an infidelity by Bloom (who, after all, never touches her) but as the sign of a possible return by Bloom to Molly and to fertile sexuality. This link represents a particularly ironic application of Gerty's role in the novel, since it forms no part of Gerty's own fantasies, and since more severe readers and critics interpret Bloom's encounter with Gerty as a largely negative or even disgusting event. In fact, it need be nothing of the kind. Both episodes, 'Nausicaa' and 'Penelope', are also introspective and static, with little external action apart from the self-stimulation of Bloom and Gerty in 'Nausicaa', which parallels the orgasmic conclusion of Molly's monologue. Moreover, 'Nausicaa' begins with Bloom's actual contemplation of Howth ('dear old Howth guarding as ever the waters of the bay', in the fulsome language of the episode's opening paragraph [13/4]), and 'Penelope' ends with Molly's emotional recollection of Howth, a place sacred in the romantic lives of both Bloom and Molly. 'Nausicaa' begins at sunset and so opens the nocturnal half of *Ulysses*, whereas 'Penelope' takes place in the early hours of the next morning, and seems to herald the dawn (Molly gives more thought to the new day than any other character).

'Sirens' anticipates and prepares for 'Nausicaa' in several respects. Female exhibitionism and male ogling mark both episodes, but by comparison with the customers' crassly flirtatious and condescending treatment of the barmaids, Bloom's behaviour towards Gerty seems almost gracious.

'Sirens' evokes pent-up erotic frustration, for which 'Nausi-caa' provides (partly comic) relief, but this comparison must be qualified by correlations and contrasts between Bloom and Molly: her liaison with Boylan is consummated, offstage, between the two episodes. The plaintive aspect of Bloom's feelings and behaviour in 'Nausicaa', then, is reinforced by the link with 'Sirens'. Both episodes emphasise Bloom's solitude, sadness, and tendency to escapism.

Apart from 'Proteus', the episode with the closest affinities to 'Nausicaa' is 'Lotus Eaters'. Joyce includes a number of detailed links in plot and phrasing to reinforce the thematic associations. Bloom remembers in 'Nausicaa' that he had forgotten to return to the chemist to collect the lotion which he had ordered for Molly in 'Lotus Eaters': 'Never went back and the soap not paid' (13/1045). Both episodes also contain references to makeup, a preoccupation of Molly's and, es-pecially, of Gerty's. After the masturbation in 'Nausicaa' Bloom recalls with satisfaction that he had resisted the temptation to masturbate in 'Lotus Eaters': 'Damned glad I didn't do it in the bath this morning over her [Martha's] silly I will punish you letter' (13/786-7). (This pattern, of arousal and partial fulfilment, recalls the link between 'Nausicaa' and 'Sirens'.) Bloom's recollection of Martha's letter in the present context in 'Nausicaa' associates the pseudonymous Martha with Gerty, and Bloom even wonders briefly if the two women might be the same person (13/944). This hypothesis will strike most readers as unlikely, but then we know far more about Gerty than Bloom does; and we have less reason than Bloom might have to seek congruities among his various erotic distractions. Martha and Gerty both represent for Bloom safely distant (if partial) means of sexual consolation, and both seem as likely to direct him back to Molly as to confirm or accentuate his estrangement from her. Both 'Lotus Eaters' and 'Nausicaa' nevertheless remind us that Bloom often takes refuge in voyeuristic encounters as a way of evading closer contact; Bloom's observation about Gerty, at whose legs he has just gazed adoringly, 'Will she [look back]? Watch! Watch! See!' (13/936), precisely recalls his thought about the woman he ogled in 'Lotus Eaters': 'Watch! Watch! Silk flash rich stockings white. Watch!' (5/130).

The episode which most emphatically and ironically demands to be associated with 'Nausicaa', however, remains 'Proteus'. This link is especially complex and fascinating; it requires us to associate Stephen with Bloom and Stephen with Gerty (of all people), to juxtapose precisely various affinities and contrasts, and to consider thematic questions which go to the heart of *Ulysses* and which cannot readily be studied by attention to any one of the novel's episodes in isolation.

Most obviously, the two episodes take place wholly in the same setting, Sandymount Strand. Bloom may be sitting on the same rock which had been visited by Stephen earlier in the day. The stick Bloom finds on the beach recalls Stephen's ashplant (which Stephen regards as a poet's trademark), especially since Bloom uses it to write in the sand, and since he finds it immediately after noticing a fragment of paper which, in turn, recalls the vampire poem Stephen wrote at the beach on a scrap torn from Deasy's letter. Given these geographical associations, Stephen's vampire poem may seem to anticipate Bloom's appearance, and 'vampire' is one of the words which pass through Stephen's mind as he regains consciousness at the end of 'Circe' and looks up to see Bloom (15/4930). Stephen's image of the 'signatures of all things' (3/2) is echoed by Bloom's observation of 'all these rocks with lines and scars and letters' (13/1261), and Stephen's reflection about the tenuousness of verbal communication, 'Who ever anywhere will read these written words?' (3/414-15), anticipates Bloom's actions after writing in the sand: 'Mr Bloom effaced the letters with his slow boot. . . . All fades. . . . He flung his wooden pen away' (13/1266-70). These actions in turn recall Stephen's observation, 'These heavy sands are language tide and wind have silted here' (3/288-9). Stephen recollects a dream involving a melon (3/365-

9), which links him to Bloom's thoughts, and Bloom recalls dreams of his own at the end of his meditation. While walking about with his eyes closed, conjuring up an imagined world of sensory deprivation, Stephen thinks 'I am getting on nicely in the dark' (3/15); whereas in 'Nausicaa' darkness more literally surrounds Bloom as the daylight fades. Stephen imagines himself falling asleep at the end of 'Proteus', and Bloom actually falls asleep at the end of 'Nausicaa'.

'Proteus' resembles 'Nausicaa' in containing numerous references to vision. The word 'gaze', a vital term in the later episode, appears portentously in the earlier one (3/38; 3/446). Stephen spends much of his time in 'Proteus' looking at things and people, but nobody (not even the otherwise inquisitive dog) apparently notices him ('Who watches me here?' he wonders vainly [3/414]). We learn in 'Hades' that Bloom has in fact seen Stephen during this time, from his position in the funeral carriage (the irony here is further complicated by the failure of Stephen's father Simon, sitting beside Bloom in the carriage and approximately sharing his point of view, to see Stephen). But 'Proteus' contains no hint of this encounter: further confirmation that Stephen does not see Bloom in the course of his walk on the beach. Thus within the text of 'Proteus' emphasis falls on a Stephen who sees but who remains invisible to others; later we learn that Bloom has nonetheless seen Stephen. These alignments and interchanges attract parody in 'Nausicaa', where Bloom earnestly watches the exhibitionistic Gerty, and Gerty, almost as earnestly, watches the grateful Bloom: there is a dedicated exchange of glances and gazes. Thus 'Proteus' depicts a process of viewing which essentially operates in only one direction, and which we associate with Stephen; while 'Nausicaa' shows a more balanced and reciprocal process of viewing, which we associate with Bloom.

Stephen can also be compared with Gerty, who for all her immaturity is about his age; both of them, in their different ways, are narcissists who posture and pose on the beach, and both think about their reflections in mirrors. Both show a similarly keen interest in the visual realm, in beauty, in the tendency of visual impressions to deceive the spectator, and in colours; though Stephen's catalogue 'Snotgreen, blue-silver, rust' (3/3) would probably not appeal to the sensibility of the Gerty who prefers 'a neat blouse of electric blue selftinted by dolly dyes (because it was expected in the *Lady's Pictorial* that electric blue would be worn)' (13/150-51), and who reflects that 'from everything in the least indelicate her finebred nature instinctively recoiled' (13/660-61). (Yet Gerty, in an unguarded moment of irritation, inadvertently echoes Stephen's words with her allusion to the 'snottynosed twins' [13/529].) Stephen seems preoccupied with mutability and flux, as does Gerty in her less cerebral style.

'Proteus' nonetheless remains a highly intellectual episode, a concatenation of abstract thoughts, for all Stephen's defer-ence towards Aristotle's empiricism and his own interest in the visual realm. Stephen's more abstruse meditations receive repeated ironic qualification in the course of Gerty's thoughts. Ironies operating in the opposite direction can, as usual in *Ulysses*, be found: Gerty's sillier or more self-indulgent reflections are often qualified by a more realistic or cynical thought expressed by Stephen. Gerty's actual and troubling lameness, we learn, results from 'an accident coming down Dalkey hill' (13/651), but she tries ineffectually to hide the consequences of this accident. This aspect of Gerty recalls Stephen's abstract but also realistic speculation about what might happen 'if [he] fell over a cliff' while walking about with his eyes closed (3/14). Stephen actually writes a poem during 'Proteus', which when we read the resulting text seems derivative but the product of some talent; Gerty, less convincingly, feels

> that she too could write poetry if she could only express
> herself like that poem that appealed to her so deeply that
> she had copied out of the newspaper she found one
> evening round the potherbs. *Art thou real, my ideal?* it was

called by Louis J Walsh, Magherafelt, and after there was something about *twilight, wilt thou ever?* and ofttimes the beauty of poetry, so sad in its transient loveliness, had misted her eyes with silent tears. (13/643-9)

Yet Gerty, a stranger, notices Bloom's actual sadness (13/370) with more astuteness and empathy than anyone else he meets during the day—including Stephen—even though she wrongly assumes that his sadness is connected with the ostensible reason for his wearing mourning.

Both Stephen in 'Proteus' and Gerty in 'Nausicaa' reflect on the constraints imposed by younger and older family members, the risk of entrapment in family circumstances like poverty and drunkenness, the jealousy, altercations and territorial disputes which may arise among siblings, friends or other contemporaries, and the need for discreetness in the performance of certain tasks ('Better get this job over quick' [3/456]; 'Behind. Perhaps there is someone' [3/502]; 'Cissy's quick motherwit guessed what was amiss and she whispered to Edy Boardman to take [Tommy] there behind the pushcar where the gentleman couldn't see and to mind he didn't wet his new tan shoes' [13/75-7]). Both characters think about love and sexuality; Gerty's gesture of displaying her legs and underwear to Bloom is ironically anticipated in Stephen's speculation about 'the virgin at Hodges Figgis' window' (3/426-7), 'Bet she wears those curse of God stays suspenders and yellow stockings, darned with lumpy wool' (3/430-32), and in his thoughts of 'lascivious men [and] a naked woman shining in her courts' (3/468-9). Yet Stephen's reflection 'She trusts me, her hand gentle, the longlashed eyes' (3/424) evokes a romantic ambience closely akin to that conjured up by Gerty even in her more fulsome moments. Stephen also imagines a church service (3/120-27) that anticipates in some detail the actual service which Gerty notices and considers in the course of 'Nausicaa'.

The indecisiveness that Bloom expresses in 'Nausicaa', especially about the wisdom of returning home, recalls similar uncertainties felt by Stephen in 'Proteus': 'He halted. I have passed the way to aunt Sara's. Am I not going there? Seems not' (3/158-9). It is also in 'Proteus' that Stephen reflects, of the tower where Mulligan oppresses him, 'I will not sleep there when this night comes' (3/276). Moreover, he expresses his decision not to return to his father's house either, and so 'Proteus' leaves him apparently homeless; the only 'home' he visits later in the novel, albeit briefly, is Bloom's.

The 'Proteus' and 'Nausicaa' episodes are also opposites in certain respects. They take place respectively at noon under a bright sun, and at dusk as the sun goes down; at high tide and at low tide. Stephen and Bloom might superficially be contrasted in a paradigm of youth and age which has obvious symbolic affinities with these details of setting.

Such a paradigm requires qualification, however. Though Bloom's rapprochement with Gerty is not, technically, consummated, it is still contact of a kind. While his voyeuristic ogling chiefly aims to secure his own pleasure, or at least relief, it also incorporates a genuine appreciation of and gratitude to Gerty. By contrast, 'Proteus' emphasises Stephen's solitude more insistently than any other episode. Amusingly, his meditations on the beach include the remark, 'A woman and a man. I see her skirties. Pinned up, I bet' (3/331), which ironically and precisely anticipates Bloom's encounter with Gerty in 'Nausicaa'; it may imply that Stephen is at a further, more voyeuristic remove from human contact than Bloom is. Yet Stephen's yearning for human and especially romantic and sexual contact is also expressed more directly and plaintively here than anywhere else in the novel: 'Touch me. Soft eyes. Soft soft soft hand. I am lonely here. O, touch me soon, now. . . . I am quiet here alone. Sad too. Touch, touch me' (3/434-6).

The association between 'Nausicaa' and 'Proteus' also leads to our next area of investigation: ironic connections between *Ulysses* and Joyce's earlier works. For one such connection, we will find, the 'Proteus'/'Nausicaa' affinities provide an especially apt paradigm: this is the association between Bloom's response to Gerty MacDowell in 'Nausicaa' and Stephen Dedalus' response to the girl on the beach in the *Portrait*. The encounter in 'Nausicaa' reacts with that shown in the earlier novel even more closely, in some respects, than it does with experiences depicted in 'Proteus'. Joyce, then, clearly meant his various works to acquire further implications through the often ironical ways in which they interact with one another in a reader's mind.

5

Ironies from Early Joyce

Beyond the ironies which link widely separated episodes of *Ulysses* are those which escape the gravitational field of the novel completely and associate sections of the text with passages in Joyce's previous prose works: *Dubliners*, *Exiles*, and especially *A Portrait of the Artist as a Young Man*. In these cases, the contexts required for revaluation of an ironic passage in Ulysses are to be found not only beyond the episode containing it, but beyond the novel; close attention to Joyce's own earlier writings, and the extent to which they do or do not form a continuum or a pattern, is required before such ironies can be fully grasped. These ironies linking apparently discrete Joyce texts, like those linking different episodes within *Ulysses*, may have thematic implications as well as structural importance. Standards of judgment valid for a given entity, Joyce reminds us, may need to be drawn not only from other portions of the entity, but from existing, cognate structures whose presence may be an unsuspected prerequisite for that of the object (or text) in question.

Some of the associations that literary history makes between *Ulysses* and each of its three antecedent texts support the notion that Joyce wished to explore ironic links among them. *Ulysses*, for example, was originally conceived as a short story to be included in the *Dubliners* collection. Joyce must have been amused, as well as pleased, when the story underwent a considerable period of gestation and growth, and at last emerged triumphantly metamorphosed into a novel vastly longer and more complex than the entire collection of stories of which it had once been envisaged as a single modest component. Embedded in *Ulysses*, as oblique hallmarks of its genesis and development, are numerous assumptions about the different scales of experience which can be addressed in a short story and in a novel. The remarkable rich aesthetic, moral and social context of *Ulysses* nurtures and energises standards of judgment and degrees of sensitivity which might have alleviated the types of depriva- tion and insufficiency anatomised in *Dubliners*, but which could scarcely be accommodated and developed within the frame of a story. *Ulysses* seems a graphic illustration of the vast quantity of 'implicit' material which a *Dubliners* story might in fact include, or which might be necessary for adequate evaluation of the experiences depicted in the stor- ies. 'The Dead' has a transitional function in incorporating as many such standards as a *Dubliners* story could plausibly contain, and in adumbrating some of the modes of *Ulysses*; as a text, it appears to undergo the same kind of philosophical expansion that Joyce himself experienced as he moved from *Dubliners* to *Ulysses*. But much of the force of 'The Dead' arises from its uniqueness, from its impressive ability to balance, counterweigh and finally transcend the fourteen earlier stories in the collection, and it could not have become a paradigm for subsequent short stories, within *Dubliners* or elsewhere. Like *Exiles*, it marks the end of Joyce's work in its particular genre; it also contains messages which could be voiced only once, and has value partly because it does so. A reader's awareness of such historical links with *Dubliners* enhances a reading of *Ulysses* by suggesting the constraints which might still limit the depiction of certain kinds of experience, even in a text by Joyce, if the intricate mecha- nisms of *Ulysses* had not evolved to help him in presenting them.

We might nonetheless notice with amusement the many ways in which, for all its bulk and amplitude, *Ulysses* still resembles a typical *Dubliners* story. The social setting of the novel recalls that of the collection of stories: lower-middle- class Dublin, concentrated largely on the north side of the Liffey. Genteel life in the south of the city mostly takes place offstage in both texts: Corley and Lenehan drift through affluent streets in 'Two Gallants' but have no real contacts there; in *Ulysses*, Stephen finds himself excluded from George Moore's plush literary evening in Ely Place—which, coincidentally or otherwise, is the setting of the final encounter in 'Two Gallants'. Most characters in both works lead similarly benighted professional and family lives.

As if to illustrate and emphasise such elements of continuity, Joyce introduces into *Ulysses* a number of particular characters whom we have previously encountered in *Dubliners*. For example, Mr Power, Martin Cunningham, Tom Kernan and C. P. M'Coy appear in the story 'Grace' and reappear in early episodes of *Ulysses*. M'Coy is seen in 'Lotus Eaters' asking Bloom to record his name on the list of mourners at Paddy Dignam's funeral, which he plans not to attend; in 'Hades', the other three characters from 'Grace' appear in the flesh at that funeral. The contrast between the group 'actually' present at Dignam's graveside and M'Coy, who is only 'fictionally' present through Bloom's willingness to record his name, seems a wry gloss on the reappearance of all these characters within *Ulysses* itself, since the only previous existence enjoyed by any of them came when they appeared in a fictional work, *Dubliners*. Lenehan from 'Two Gallants' appears several times in *Ulysses*, notably in 'Aeolus'. Especially interesting is the reappearance of Bob Doran from 'The Boarding House': in his case, we not only discover new facts which help to explain a previous, more cryptic appearance, but observe a process of change and deterioration which was already tentatively adumbrated in *Dubliners*. In 'The Boarding House' Doran foolishly allows himself to be entrapped in what will clearly become a loveless marriage; in 'Cyclops' we see him seeking alcoholic consolation for an unhappy home life, and comforting himself with rationalisations for those same inadequacies in his own character which had been presented for our inspection in *Dubliners*. Bantam Lyons, who appears several times in *Ulysses*, had likewise been mentioned by name in 'The Boarding House'.

Also notable are the recollections in *Ulysses* of several *Dubliners* characters who do not actually appear in the novel: Bartell D'Arcy, Gabriel and Gretta Conroy, and Kate and Julia Morkan, all from 'The Dead'; and Mrs Sinico from 'A Painful Case'. (The remarkably numerous characters recalled from 'The Dead' help to confirm our sense of its status as a special and definitive story, and our awareness that one of its functions, bestowed on it by Joyce retrospectively as he worked on the later novel, is to link *Dubliners* to *Ulysses*.) Kate Morkan is unexpectedly identified in *Ulysses* as Stephen's godmother (17/139-40), and we now learn of the death of Julia Morkan, which had been anticipated in 'The Dead' by Gabriel Conroy. If, as seems likely, 'The Dead' is set on 6 January 1904, only five months before the date of *Ulysses*, Julia's death must indeed have occurred 'very soon' after the party depicted in 'The Dead', as Gabriel had anticipated (*D* 222-3). Stephen, of course, plays no part in *Dubliners*. But if *Dubliners* and *Ulysses* are consistent in their naturalistic intermeshings, and Joyce implies that they are, Stephen Dedalus must almost certainly have met Gabriel Conroy at his godmother's house. Gabriel must, in turn, have been at least slightly known to the Blooms, since Molly has asked Bloom questions about Gabriel's wife Gretta: 'What had Gretta Conroy on?' (4/522). Thus a further association, never mentioned explicitly in *Ulysses*, links Stephen and Bloom; and we need to know the text of *Dubliners* in order to detect it. Bloom, we learn in *Ulysses*, had attended Mrs Sinico's funeral, even though Bloom himself never appears in *Dubliners*, and it is difficult to imagine him there (6/996-7; 17/945-8). (This perceived gap between Bloom and the characters of *Dubliners* finds a faint echo in Bloom's social isolation in Dublin, as *Ulysses* depicts it, and perhaps even in his habit of attending the funerals of people he has scarcely known, like Dignam and Mrs Sinico.) Bloom, for all his richness of personality, is nonetheless the same kind of person as most characters in the story collection: an advertisement canvasser who is not especially good at or interested in his not especially demanding job, ineffectual and troubled in his domestic circumstances, and prone to compensate by acts of evasion and substitution for his feelings of inadequacy; he has vague, unrealised aspirations to literary expression and cultural fulfilment which recall the yearnings detectable in *Dubliners* characters like James Duffy and Little Chandler.

Ulysses also resembles a *Dubliners* story in its time-span, its plot, and even its themes. The eighteen-hour period in which all the events of *Ulysses* are concentrated seems remarkably brief for such an expansive novel (though the time-span of *Finnegans Wake* is similar). It would be adequate to contain the incidents depicted in many of the *Dubliners* stories, such as 'After the Race', 'Counterparts', 'Clay', 'Two Gallants' or 'The Dead', though some of the stories do treat a considerably longer period, notably 'A Painful Case'. The plot of *Ulysses* remains in bald outline (for all its elaborate ramifications) no more complex than that of a typical *Dubliners* story, and the novel's resolution and meaning, like those of many of the stories, depend more upon moments of revelation than on events. Crucial in *Ulysses* is a change in perceptions within a marital relationship, a change which depends on the disturbance of that relationship by an outsider: this development has analogies with typical plots presented in *Dubliners*, notably that of 'The Dead'. Although *Ulysses* obviously permits much greater thematic richness and exfoliation than do the *Dubliners* stories, its main thematic preoccupations remain straightforward enough: for example, it seeks to depict the inadequacies of personal and social relationships that lack kindness and affection.

Ulysses also seems an ironic parody of the *Dubliners* collection as a whole. *Dubliners* mimes in its total structure the kinds of disjunctiveness and alienation which the individual stories depict in detail: for example, through the method of showing repeatedly the same parts of society but ensuring that no important individual character appears in more than one story. The fragmentation thus evoked through a series of fifteen discrete stories serves as a paradigm for some of Joyce's structural decisions in *Ulysses* as well. The transition from the third to the fourth episode of *Ulysses*, when we move from Stephen to Bloom, is as startling and disjunctive as that between any of the neighbouring stories in *Dubliners*, even that between 'Grace' and 'The Dead'. In its latter stages *Ulysses* mimes fragmentation through its radical changes and experiments in literary style, so that even where two consecutive episodes depict the same group of characters, the episodes in question will diverge strikingly in their manner of doing so, and will thus remind us that analogous situations may look markedly different from varying points of view — a theme which remains a persistent concern in *Dubliners* as well.

The early episodes of *Ulysses* recall the early stories of *Dubliners* in several specific ways. In both books, an opening triad of stories or episodes embodies a youthful male sensibility and a series of responses to experience which later portions of the book will progressively qualify. Joyce described the first three stories in *Dubliners* as 'stories of *my* childhood' (*L II* 111, italics added), and evidence can be found to support the autobiographical implications of this remark. The boy narrators of the three stories (who may all be the same boy, though evidence for this hypothesis is deliberately withheld by the text, presumably to reinforce our sense of the protagonists' solitude and the disjunctiveness of experience) all live with an aunt and uncle who resemble Joyce's parents (and Stephen Dedalus' parents), reside at actual addresses where Joyce himself had once lived, and undergo several particular experiences whose details can be traced to Joyce's biography. Thus these narrators, in their quieter way, have a relationship to Joyce's present narrating self which closely resembles the relationship between Stephen Dedalus, as he appears early in *Ulysses*, and the Joyce describing him. Particular analogies between the personalities of these boys and of Stephen himself can also be discovered. The boy narrators supply to the opening phase of *Dubliners* an artistic, articulate, questioning, introspective and solipsistic spirit, similar to the mood established at the beginning of *Ulysses* by the thoughts and words of Stephen Dedalus.

We can find particular analogies between the individual stories in *Dubliners* and individual, 'corresponding' episodes in *Ulysses*. For example, the second *Dubliners* story 'An Encounter' and the second *Ulysses* episode 'Nestor' both feature school settings, a schoolmaster ineffectually drilling his often rebellious pupils in rote learning, and an encounter between a sadistic older man and a young bookish male — who in each case recognises the depravity of the older one but treats him with apparent respect. We might even associate the flawed priest James Flynn in the first *Dubliners* story 'The Sisters', who is viewed as a potentially dangerous influence on the young narrator, with the mock-priest Mulligan in the first *Ulysses* episode 'Telemachus', who seems a potentially dangerous influence on Stephen. (Giorgio Melchiori has suggested that Joyce's depiction of Mulligan as 'stately' and 'plump' recalls his account of Flynn as 'solemn and copious' [Melchiori 125].)

The stories in the central portion of *Dubliners* — essentially, those from 'Eveline' to 'Grace' — are analogous in several senses to the episodes in the mid-section of *Ulysses* from 'Calypso' to 'Circe'. In both books, these central stories or episodes follow sections which have been coloured by youthful anxiety or discontent, and illustrate various (yet often ineffectual) antidotes or qualifications which might be sought in response to the moods depicted in those earlier sections. They are set in places like streets, offices, committee rooms, pubs and restaurants. The central portions of both texts thus concern themselves with the realms of 'mature' (but often seriously inadequate) relationships and of 'public life': the mid-range daylight world and its discontents. Characters in successive *Dubliners* stories frequently become 'counterparts' of one another, and so do the characters who appear in the successive episodes of *Ulysses*.

Especially striking are the analogies between the final story of *Dubliners*, 'The Dead', and the concluding phase of *Ulysses* — the Nostos, particularly its last episode, 'Penelope'. In both texts, there is an emphatic return to the personal and introspective, after the objective and public emphases of the central section; and there is a motif of 'homecoming', as Gabriel and Gretta travel to their room after the party and Bloom returns to his house and to Molly's bed. Gabriel and Gretta turn to the past in their thoughts and consequently confront anew certain aspects and problems of their relationship; Molly's thoughts return eventually to Bloom, but only after an energetic exploration of alternatives to him. Gabriel's reconsideration of his marriage follows the intrusion into Gretta's thoughts of her former lover Michael; Bloom's reconsideration of his marriage follows the intrusion into Molly's thoughts and life of her new lover Boylan. In both cases, the husband acknowledges the importance of other realities besides himself in the life of his wife, with a detachment from immediate and selfish concerns which few other characters in either *Dubliners* or *Ulysses* would be able to achieve. Gabriel and Bloom both remain flawed, but they are Joyce's two most appealing male characters, and both appear at their best in their moments of self-denial and recognition of their wives' autonomy. Both *Dubliners* and *Ulysses* end with one partner in the marriage awake meditating while the other rests or sleeps. In both cases Joyce shows a contrast between male and female perspectives, and dramatises future possibilities by using images and symbols suggesting oceans and travel, separation, estrangement, dissolution, revaluation and reconciliation. Both *Dubliners* and *Ulysses* end with the infusion of a female perspective, something that has been largely missing in earlier portions of both texts (with occasional local exceptions, such as those provided by the central character in 'Eveline' and by Gerty MacDowell in 'Nausicaa'), and with a return to lyricism, acceptance, and mutuality. The two texts, 'The Dead' and *Ulysses*, both imply strongly that the day whose events they depict has been crucial in the lives of the characters. *Exiles* and *Finnegans Wake*, and to some extent 'Eveline' and the *Portrait*, all end similarly, but with less resolution.

Joyce's play *Exiles* also has significant links to *Ulysses* in terms of literary history. Joyce had always shown a keen interest in drama and its theoretical possibilities, but had not written a 'mature' play. Yet once he had begun drafting *Ulysses*, he obviously felt an obligation to explore some of his current thematic preoccupations in an uncompromisingly dramatic form: he set his *Ulysses* manuscript aside, wrote *Exiles* and attempted to arrange for its performance and its translation into several other languages, and only then returned to his work on the text of *Ulysses*. It therefore seems clear that *Exiles* represented for Joyce a necessary introduction to or phase of the experience which is centrally embodied in *Ulysses*: an exploration or 'staging' of certain characters, situations, actions and conflicts which needed to be shaped for fiction by preliminary exposure to the rigorous objectivity of the stage. Joyce seemingly wanted to test material analogous to that contemplated for *Ulysses* in a raw setting, free of narrative support and humour, before treating it more urbanely in the novel itself. Whereas characters in *Dubliners* and the *Portrait* often appear in isolation, the dramatic structure of *Exiles* ensures that interaction among characters becomes an almost constant preoccupation, as it will remain in *Ulysses* as well. And since as a play it consists almost wholly of dialogue, *Exiles* further acts as a prelude for *Ulysses* by permitting the expression of various views of apposite topics, most obviously adultery; thus it helps to prepare for the cryptic silences of *Ulysses* on such subjects. In other words, Joyce could be reticent about certain topics in *Ulysses* partly because he had already had them discussed by the characters in *Exiles*.

Knowledge of the place of *Exiles* within the pattern of Joyce's work also assists a reading of *Ulysses* by refining our sense both of his general concept of the dramatic and of the particular modes of experience which he thought were best suited to dramatic expression. *Exiles*, moreover, operates as an ironic gloss on *Ulysses*, notably by presenting in stylised and heightened form the excessively romantic or self-aggrandising modes of behaviour on which the novel also sometimes concentrates.

Exiles shares with *Ulysses* a preoccupation with certain character-types and thematic concerns: the mature man, the sensual man, the earthy wife, and the concepts of (potential or actual) cuckoldry, doubt and jealousy, uncertainty, and spiritual exile. As a potential marital distraction, Beatrice Justice in *Exiles* seems plaintive, attenuated and ineffectual. She closely anticipates, in these respects, Martha Clifford in *Ulysses*. Richard Rowan in *Exiles* resembles the Stephen Dedalus of *Ulysses* in several ways; each of these characters, for example, has recently returned to Dublin after a period of exile, and feels aloof and alienated there. We notice that Richard, like Stephen, has neglected a 'dying wish' of his mother's and consequently feels racked by guilt. Robert Hand seems to play in Richard's life a role analogous to the roles of Cranly, Lynch and Mulligan in Stephen's life: a friend who sometimes behaves like a disciple willing to betray his master. But Richard has also assimilated a few features which seem more characteristic of Leopold Bloom. He may represent an attempt by Joyce to graft some Bloomian attributes onto the figure of Stephen before turning to treat Stephen and Bloom as separate entities in *Ulysses*. Richard's notion of the way in which a man should love a woman, by aiming especially 'to wish her well' (*E* 79), resembles Bloom's view. The centrality of the Richard/Bertha relationship in *Exiles* anticipates that of the Bloom/Molly relationship in *Ulysses*; and in both cases, we feel that external threats to this central relationship, especially as embodied in the 'male rivals' Robert and Boylan, will probably be overcome. Some of Robert's attributes, like his earthiness, reappear in Bloom, as if to show that such features may sometimes be susceptible to assimilation, rather than requiring to be conquered. The female perspective seems dominant for the moment at the end of *Exiles*, as it does at the end of *Ulysses*. Yet both endings also emphasise inconclusiveness and uncertainty in terms of future events, and our hope for a positive outcome cannot in either case find much specific support in the text.

Such literary-historical links between *Ulysses* and earlier works by Joyce are most obvious and comprehensive in the case of *A Portrait of the Artist as a Young Man*. Joyce had originally intended to end that novel by depicting Stephen's symbolic territorial struggles in the Martello tower with a character resembling Buck Mulligan. His act of embarking on *Ulysses*, and his decision to begin this later novel with the Martello tower scene, considerably reshaped the ending of the *Portrait*, from which Mulligan was summarily excluded. The decision helped in turn to determine the apparently positive conclusion to the *Portrait*, in which Stephen's resolution to explore 'life' on the Continent is not specifically, ironically undermined within the text of the novel, even though it is essentially the same kind of experience whose limitations the *Portrait* has earlier set itself to delineate. Joyce may have depicted Stephen's aspirations without ironic safeguards (and in Stephen's own fulsome but endearingly positive language in the *Portrait* diary) because he had now formulated a strategy of radical ironic qualification involving the associations between the two novels. *Ulysses* works to undermine the conclusion to the *Portrait* as each of that novel's chapters had undermined its predecessor, but does so much more radically, and it offers a complexity of response to experience which leaves the *Portrait* far behind. Joyce demonstrably intended the *Portrait* to serve as a preliminary text available to all readers of *Ulysses*: he always attempted to ensure that when *Ulysses* was to be translated into a particular language, the *Portrait* should appear in that language first. He also rivets the books together by incorporating into the early episodes of *Ulysses* a number of allusions (such as the reference to Stephen's friend Cranly) which can be glossed only by study of the *Portrait*: no other primary text or source, anywhere, can explain such allusions.

Two particularly specific and intense ironic connections link the *Portrait* and *Ulysses*. Bloom's encounter with Gerty MacDowell on the beach in 'Nausicaa' (which is in many ways a positive experience, but also tainted by narcissistic, delusory and farcical connotations) undermines in retrospect Stephen's apparently sublime and artistic vision of the bird-girl on the beach at the end of the fourth chapter of the *Portrait*. And the ending of the *Portrait*, which shows Stephen's seemingly triumphant escape from the constraining forces of Ireland, interacts bleakly with the first three episodes of *Ulysses*. In those episodes Stephen, having returned to Ireland after making his escape, seems more seriously troubled and constrained than he had been at any time in the earlier novel.

Bloom's ogling of Gerty elaborately, parodically and ironically recapitulates Stephen's contemplation of the bird-girl. In both cases the setting is a beach at dusk, with observer and observed remaining static throughout the central part of the incident, and with the observer falling asleep (in a mood of euphoria, or at least of grateful relief) at the end of the scene. The observer in each case is male, solitary and unknown to the observed, who is in each case female, largely anonymous, and essentially solitary at the most vital stage of the scene (though Gerty MacDowell is addressed by name in Bloom's hearing, and she is encumbered by her friends and the group of children at first—a situation anticipated in the mention, early in the description of the encounter in the *Portrait*, of 'children and girls and voices childish and girlish in the air' (*P* 171; all quotations from the *Portrait* given in the next three paragraphs are from this page).

Stephen offers the girl 'the worship of his eyes' and, as he watches her, experiences 'an outburst of profane joy'; Bloom seems to Gerty to be 'literally worshipping at her shrine' (13/ 564) and is placed in a setting outside a church denoted as 'that simple fane beside the waves' (13/286), in which a service of worship is currently in progress. Senn draws attention to this association, as to many other links between the two scenes, pointing out in particular that 'profane' means literally 'outside the temple' (Hart and Hayman 286). This link confirms that Joyce had Stephen's 'profane joy' prominently in mind as he worked apposite words and phrases into the text of the 'Nausicaa' episode. Both scenes contain insistent references to eyes, gazing, and especially the mutuality of the process of contemplation: in each case, the female participant becomes aware of the attention of the male, turns her gaze from a distant view of the sea, and responds in kind, staring back without shame. The bird-girl at first appears 'gazing out to sea'; but 'when she felt his presence and the worship of his eyes her eyes turned to him in quiet sufferance of his gaze, without shame or wantonness. Long, long she suffered his gaze'. Gerty, seen first 'gazing far away into the distance' (13/80), then 'gazed out towards the distant sea' (13/406). She has become aware of 'the gentleman opposite looking' (13/365), however, and they have 'exchanged glances' (13/367). Gerty now 'looked at him a moment, meeting his glance' (13/690). Gerty reflects on 'the face that met her gaze there in the twilight' (13/368-9), realising that 'it was her he was looking at, and there was meaning in his look' (13/411-12). Bloom is 'fascinated by a loveliness that made him gaze' (13/541); 'he could see and he was looking all the time' (13/557-8).

Both girls are described in similarly ambivalent terms, which speak approvingly of purity but simultaneously manage in both cases to evoke considerable erotic power. The bird-girl's 'long slender bare legs were delicate. . . . Her thighs, fuller and softhued as ivory, were bared almost to the hips where the white fringes of her drawers were like featherings of soft white down. Her slateblue skirts were kilted boldly about her waist. . . . Her bosom was as a bird's soft and slight, slight and soft'. Gerty's figure, similarly, is 'slight and graceful' (13/83) and her face has an 'ivorylike purity' (13/88); she wears a blue skirt but also wears white; and she displays her 'shapely limbs' (13/170) fully and candidly to her observer. The bird-girl stirs the water with her foot 'hither and thither'; the latter phrase appears three times in four lines, setting up an insistently sexual rhythm. In 'Nausicaa' the bat, which is associated with Gerty as birds are associated with the girl in the *Portrait*, echoes this phrase as it flies 'hither, thither, with a tiny lost cry' (13/626-7) — this cry anticipating the orgasmic cry attributed to Gerty later, 'that cry that has rung through the ages' (13/736), as well as recalling the cry of profane joy uttered by Stephen's soul in the *Portrait*. The hither-and-thither movement of the bird-girl's foot, still more strikingly, foreshadows Gerty's gesture of swinging her foot and then her leg: 'she just swung her foot in and out in time' (13/498-9); 'she swung her leg more in and out in time' (13/557). (The phrase 'to and fro' [13/719], applied to one of the fireworks, further reinforces the sexual rhythm here.) Gerty's leg-swinging gesture at once echoes the gesture of the bird-girl, supports and enhances Gerty's exhibitionistic display, reciprocally imitates and intensifies the rhythm of Bloom's masturbation, and touchingly evokes the pathos of Gerty's lameness: her legs serve her well enough when she displays or swings them, but will fail to do so as soon as she attempts to walk.

More generally, Gerty's self-image, so obviously and pathetically inflated to compensate for her lameness and her miserable home circumstances, seems to be anticipated by the account of Stephen's inner life which appears in the *Portrait* immediately before he sees the bird-girl: his soul, he reflects, would 'brood alone upon the shame of her wounds and in her house of squalor and subterfuge to queen it'. The scenes in both novels also appear highly coloured and 'staged', pictorial, theatrical or operatic, and phrases taken from the thoughts of Gerty and those of Bloom appear to provide an ironic gloss not only on the immediate setting in 'Nausicaa' but on the encounter in the *Portrait* as well: Gerty reflects, on an actual 'picture of halcyon days', that 'you could see there was a story behind it. The colours were done something lovely' (13/334-8); and Bloom believes, when he thinks about female courting or sexual behaviour, that a woman feels she 'must have the stage setting, the rouge, costume, position, music' (13/855-6). Bloom's thoughts of 'those girls, those girls, those lovely seaside girls' (13/906) wryly recall not only the present setting, Gerty and her friends, and Boylan's song, but Stephen's vision of the bird-girl.

Moreover, as Senn points out, the encounter in 'Nausicaa' ironically qualifies its counterpart in the *Portrait* through its verbal links to that earlier scene: 'The purple tinge, noticeable in [the] *Portrait*, but not easily appreciated with critical nicety, has now been applied much more strongly. One's impressions of the earlier scene will now be readjusted; in the comic exaggerations of "Nausicaa" some traits in [the] *Portrait* are seen in a different light' (Hart and Hayman 286). Yet the relationship between the two scenes may be more nearly reciprocal than this account implies: although presumably Joyce had not foreseen the 'Nausicaa' episode in any detail when he wrote the scene in the *Portrait*, he must nonetheless have been keenly aware of the kind of external ironical qualification to which the bird-girl scene might be susceptible. It is possible that he withheld more intense internal ironic qualification, of a kind that could have been supplied within the *Portrait* itself, as this opportunity occurred to him; if so, this deferment of the ironic rejoinder resembles the mode adopted at the end of the fifth chapter of the *Portrait*, where Joyce demonstrably decided to withhold the rejoinder and to have it appear in his subsequent text, *Ulysses*.

In any case, it is valid to claim that the scene in the *Portrait* provides an ironic qualification of the scene in *Ulysses*, as well as to recognise the more apparent qualification operating in the opposite direction. As we juxtapose the two scenes, we may also observe that the 'artistic' dimension of Stephen's contemplation of the bird-girl (which is a little exaggerated and lush, but not therefore absurd) implies that there is a similarly artistic component in Bloom's contemplation of Gerty, which should be taken seriously. The encounter between Bloom and Gerty has value for both participants, and though Bloom is realistic about its limitations, he is genuinely appreciative of and grateful to Gerty; for all the oddity of the encounter, he reflects rather movingly, 'still it was a kind of language between us' (13/944). In the *Portrait*, similarly, the bird-girl's response to Stephen's gaze suggests that each participant appreciates the presence of the other. A kind of reciprocity thus links the two texts at this point in the development of each of them; and it faintly recalls the reciprocal acts of gazing by the characters which are recounted specifically within the text in both cases.

The relationship between the ending of the *Portrait* and the opening of *Ulysses* operates in a still more emphatically ironic manner. This link has a number of ironic dimensions, but it seems best here to concentrate on the most central one: the association between Stephen's plan to free himself as an artist by leaving Ireland, recounted at the end of the *Portrait*, and its qualification in the depiction of his entrapped state after his premature return to Ireland, at the beginning of *Ulysses*.

Towards the end of the *Portrait*, Stephen expresses a fragmentary manifesto, both in the course of conversation with friends (especially Cranly) and in his diary. His plans and proclamations do attract a modest degree of ironic qualification within the *Portrait* itself, partly because Cranly's personality and circumstances make him especially well-equipped to query the more vulnerable parts of Stephen's discourse, and partly because the prosaic contours of a diary (a form of expression which Joyce himself never practised) seem ill-suited to Stephen's more fanciful declarations. (The effect of these internal ironies is slightly muted by the diary's demonstration of Stephen's own developing capacity for self-criticism and even self-mockery: 'O, give it up, old chap! Sleep it off!' [*P* 252].) Yet the *Portrait* ends positively enough.

If *Ulysses* did not exist, readers of the earlier novel would have little substantial evidence with which to qualify Stephen's statements at the end of the *Portrait*.

We do need, however, to bring *Ulysses* into the picture since, in its depiction of Stephen, it clearly functions as a sequel to the *Portrait*. And once *Ulysses* is considered, the Stephen of the diary and of the conversations with Cranly appears to change considerably. The alterations are not exclusively negative: the Stephen of *Ulysses* seems in some respects a more impressive person than the earlier one, even if he has failed to develop in the manner anticipated in the *Portrait*. Like other Joycean ironies, moreover, these links between the two novels operate in both directions: the Stephen of the *Portrait* qualifies his counterpart of *Ulysses* just as the latter Stephen qualifies his predecessor. The detailed operation of these ironies doubtless owes much to the facts of literary history: Joyce had planned many aspects of *Ulysses* at the time he wrote the fifth chapter of the *Portrait* and revised the earlier chapters. He sets up an intriguing ironic interplay between the two texts which enriches both of them. We can say that the *Portrait* would be a different novel if *Ulysses* had never been written, just as *Ulysses* would be different without the *Portrait*.

In the *Portrait* Stephen declares resonantly to Cranly:

> I will not serve that in which I no longer believe whether it call itself my home, my fatherland or my church: and I will try to express myself in some mode of life or art as freely as I can and as wholly as I can, using for my defence the only arms I allow myself to use—silence, exile, and cunning. (*P* 246-7)

The opening of *Ulysses* seems designed to qualify these grandiloquent aspirations with pointed specificity. Stephen has obviously expressed some of his ambitions to Mulligan, who teases him mercilessly about them in 'Telemachus'. Mulligan, for all his facile blasphemy and his veneer of non-conformity, is at ease with institutions, with home and fatherland and church. He is anything but silent, imposing constant banter onto Stephen (so reducing Stephen to a state of 'silence', but not in the volitional manner he had sought). Mulligan might take a brief, opportunistic (and un-Odyssean) trip to Greece but would see no need for a longer 'exile' from Ireland. For all Mulligan's cleverness and wit, he also seems incapable of 'cunning' in Stephen's subtler sense.

Thus Stephen, having departed decisively and eloquently from Ireland at the end of the *Portrait*, returns at the beginning of *Ulysses* to confront a person who embodies the antitheses of most of the values he had exiled himself to pursue, and who now threatens to taint him with the temptation to compromise or abandon those values. Stephen's forced retreat into silence seems to leave him vulnerable rather than strong; his attempt at exile has apparently failed; and his cunning does not suffice to protect him from his antagonistic environment. Mulligan reminds Stephen that he still bears within him the 'cursed jesuit strain' (1/209); having left his father's house, Stephen now feels he must leave Mulligan's house as well, a realisation which must qualify the value of the earlier departure; and Stephen's resented employment at Mr Deasy's school shows that he has failed to free himself from paternal figures and institutions. The death of his mother has left him more forlorn than liberated, and he still feels in danger of 'drowning' if he allows himself any contact with his siblings, as he shows in his response to the meeting with his sister Dilly in 'Wandering Rocks'.

At the end of the *Portrait* Stephen proudly declares, 'I do not fear to be alone' (*P* 247). In 'Proteus', however, he finds his own moments of solitude mostly depressing and unproductive, as we are reminded in a passage already quoted in Chapter 4: 'I am lonely here. O, touch me soon, now. . . . I am quiet here alone. Sad too. Touch, touch me' (3/434-6). In the *Portrait* he had told his friend Davin that 'the shortest way to Tara was *via* Holyhead' (*P* 250); but in the later novel he acknowledges that his actual itinerary has been more banal, less poetic and less triumphant: 'Newhaven-Dieppe, steerage passenger. Paris and back' (9/953). His earlier plans to fly like Daedalus have been disappointed, and have led him to a new and more modest identification: 'Lapwing. Icarus. *Pater, ait.* Seabedabbled, fallen, weltering. Lapwing you are. Lapwing be' (9/953-4). Again, the *Portrait* had already included some mild ironic qualification of Stephen's Daedalian dreams. An example of such qualification is provided by Stephen's schoolmates who dive into the sea, in Icarus fashion, just as he begins musing about Daedalus and envisaging him as a symbolic paternal figure. Since Daedalus had a son who fell to his death in the sea as a result of his pride, this choric offstage splashing has a certain ironic impact. In *Ulysses*, the plump Mulligan's dive into the sea—made shortly after he flutters 'his hands at his sides like . . . wings of one about to rise in the air' (1/594-5)—will have still greater ironic impact.

In his diary Stephen lyrically anticipates 'the spell of arms and voices: the white arms of roads, their promise of close embraces and the black arms of tall ships that stand against the moon, their tale of distant nations' (*P* 252). In *Ulysses* the only roads he sees are those of Dublin, and the arms of ships anticipate his vision of the 'threemaster' at the end of 'Proteus'. This ship, its 'sails brailed up on the crosstrees' (3/504), resembles a crucifixion tableau, and the word 'three-master' recalls the three 'masters' to which Stephen acknowledges his continued subservience in 'Telemachus': 'The imperial British state . . . and the holy Roman catholic and apostolic church' (1/643-4), as well as the 'third [master] who wants me for odd jobs' (1/641), the latter being Ireland (especially as embodied in people like Mulligan and Deasy). It also seems relevant to Stephen's vision of ships expressed at the end of the *Portrait* that in *Ulysses* he arranges to meet Mulligan at a pub called the Ship, but chooses not to keep the appointment: a modest act of liberation.

Stephen also reports in his diary that, before his departure for the Continent, 'Mother is putting my new secondhand clothes in order' (*P* 252), thus implicitly suggesting that he hopes his exile will free him from parental intrusions and from his dependence and poverty. In 'Telemachus', however, Stephen wears the oppressive Mulligan's second-hand clothes, and seems to be more dependent and more afflicted by poverty than ever. Mulligan, having once declared in front of Stephen, with consummate insensitivity, that Stephen's mother May Dedalus was *'beastly dead'* (1/198-9), now hypocritically espouses sentimental notions of filial obligation: 'You could have knelt down . . . when your dying mother asked you' (1/91-2). Mulligan thus aligns himself, belatedly and insincerely, with Stephen's mother. Whereas Stephen had accused himself in the *Portrait* of 'still harping on the mother' (*P* 250), it is now Mulligan who does so; and he has far less reason for adopting this manner than Stephen had.

Stephen leaves the *Portrait* with the declaration 'Welcome, O life!' and the plan 'to encounter for the millionth time the reality of experience and to forge in the smithy of my soul the uncreated conscience of my race' (*P* 252-3). His 'Parable of the Plums', recounted in 'Aeolus', shows that he has moved towards the fulfilment of this hope, at least by writing literary texts which embody it; on the other hand, there is little sign in the episode that his audience pays much attention to his story, even though it is one of the more sympathetic audiences which Dublin might have provided for him. Bloom hears Stephen recite the same story in 'Ithaca', but again seems a largely unimpressed listener, despite his impulse to sympathise with Stephen. Once we meet Bloom, we feel that for all his flaws he appears to be more capable of understanding 'life' than Stephen is; and this impression will be confirmed with particular insistence and poignancy when the two characters talk together in 'Eumaeus' and 'Ithaca', since in these conversations Stephen seems to show little interest in understanding Bloom. Even Molly has an intuitive understanding of life which would elude Stephen. Joyce reminds us of this contrast, and neatly links the beginning of the *Portrait* to the conclusion of *Ulysses*, through a series of allusions to roses. Early in the *Portrait*, Stephen's evolving sense of duality and antithesis often finds representation in colour contrasts among flowers, a pattern which culminates in the white and red roses used to designate the competing class teams at Clongowes (*P* 12). 'Penelope' ends with several recollections by Molly of the song 'Shall I Wear a White Rose or Shall I Wear a Red?', including one which appears only six lines from the end of the episode: 'when I put the rose in my hair . . . or shall I wear a red' (18/1602-3). This association between the novels is slight, but we might notice that Molly's concern with red and white roses seems more social, more concerned with affection and less with conflict, than Stephen's.

It is Stephen's solipsism in the *Portrait* which the later novel most insistently works to qualify. In the *Portrait*, the structure as well as the themes of the novel ensure that Stephen retains an often claustrophobic degree of unapproachable centrality and isolation. In *Ulysses*, despite his occasional loneliness, he also appears at times beset and trammelled by his unavoidable contacts with other people. He is first seen from outside, and from the point of view of the domineering Mulligan; he seems central in only four of the 18 episodes; and he is qualified by the presence of many diverse characters who seem to equal or exceed his capabilities in numerous ways. Stephen's background now appears to merge with the backgrounds of various other people, and those people are joined to each other by associations which often circumvent and exclude Stephen, as we see in Bloom's contact with Simon Dedalus. *Ulysses* suggests that the process of growth in Stephen which the *Portrait* depicted has reached a plateau, but is not yet complete, and that there are many flaws in the character Stephen has so far become. For further growth, the novel shows, Stephen will have to go outside the personality he has hitherto been. His ideas will also need qualification.

Stephen's thoughts about beauty, expressed in the *Portrait*, largely ignore the problem of his ugly actual environment, though they may appear to us to arise as an unconscious response to that environment. His aesthetic also seems rather disembodied, neglectful of the human dimensions of art in terms of both creation and content. In *Ulysses*, Stephen cannot so blithely emancipate himself from the reality of his context, and some of its ugliness is ironically internalised (in the form of Stephen's rotting teeth, for example). Stephen's meditations on the development of art through lyric, epic and dramatic stages also seem qualified ironically by the total structure of *Ulysses* at least as much as they were qualified by that of the *Portrait*: the opening of *Ulysses*, where Mulligan acts out his black mass atop the Martello tower and mutters imprecations to a Stephen who is consciously posturing as Hamlet, could scarcely be more dramatic; the mid-section of *Ulysses* has an epic tone, as if to confirm the plausibility of Stephen's paradigm but also to recall the possibility of reversing its direction; Molly's soliloquy at the end of the novel could scarcely be more lyrical. (*Finnegans Wake* also appears to begin dramatically and end lyrically.) In *Ulysses* Stephen does seem consciously aware of the need to modify his earlier theories about art, and in 'Scylla and Charybdis' his concentration on the autobiographical dimensions of literary creation shows an honest attempt to correct an imbalance in those theories.

Joyce, finally, seems to have linked Stephen's experiences in the two novels, comically as well as ironically, through the domestic scenes which both texts contain, and specifically through the 'kitchen scenes'. In the *Portrait* Stephen appears in the family kitchen at several crucial moments, especially when he has become disillusioned after moments of apparent triumph (notably at the beginning of the fifth chapter). His vital encounter with Bloom in *Ulysses* takes place in the kitchen at 7 Eccles Street. This encounter, though inconclusive, does qualify the domestic scenes in the *Portrait* by suggesting possible paths of escape from the solipsism and entrapment which had been dramatised in parallel settings in the earlier novel. The setting is not merely comic nor the link merely coincidental; kitchens embody many of the domestic, familial values which Stephen needs to acknowledge. (It is appropriate that Bloom first appears to us in his kitchen.) The connection is slight, but characteristic of Joyce's impulse to work ironic associations into all the corners of his texts; and it helps to validate and clarify the larger and more abstract ironic associations which also link the two novels.

As we read *Ulysses*, then, we should keep in mind the multiple ways in which its manner differs from or enlarges on the modes of presentation used in the *Portrait*, especially in its depiction of Stephen. The ironic qualification of the earlier text which thus emerges significantly enriches a reading of *Ulysses* itself. We are also moving here towards those links to the work of other writers, and those 'ironies of the real world', which will be discussed more directly in the sixth and seventh chapters. Part of the point of the allusions to *Dubliners*, *Exiles* and the *Portrait* which Joyce includes in *Ulysses* is that the ironic targets represent experiences which have occurred previously outside the framework of the text; but in these cases, Joyce has also treated them in his earlier fiction.

We might conclude that *Ulysses* is, among many other things, an attempt to synthesise the worlds already depicted in Joyce's three completed prose works. It shares with *Dubliners* its epic, episodic, disjunctive, sequential structures and the thematic causes and consequences of those structures; like the story collection, it mostly studies cases of alienation and estrangement, showing occasional moments of mutuality or union (or 'all but union'). Like *Exiles*, it is dramatic and much concerned with conflict, and depicts a marital relationship threatened but also paradoxically aided by the presence of a male rival. It resembles the *Portrait* in its evolutionary dimension, its powers of synthesis, its lyricism, its concern with growth, and its exploration of the role of the artist.

Yet if *Ulysses* appears to fuse these modes, it remains an ironic fusion, largely concerned to show the difficulty posed by any attempt to bring them together. *Ulysses* casts new light on the constrained or constricted nature of the characters, situations and events depicted in the earlier texts, and on any aspirations to completeness which might have been expressed by those texts themselves. Only in the ampler environment of *Ulysses*, Joyce seems to say through his complex intertextual ironies, can such experiences and such aspirations approach real fulfilment.

6
Ironies from Homer and Shakespeare

Joyce incorporates into *Ulysses* many strikingly ironic links to literary texts produced by other writers, as well as associations with his own earlier works. These intertextual or 'inter-authorial' ironies might be aptly envisaged as moving in a still larger orbit outside the more local or involuted ironic cycles already discussed. One of their functions is to help situate the text of *Ulysses* dynamically (but also wryly) within those literary traditions which interested Joyce. Another is to enrich the texture of the novel by encouraging us to locate its characters, events and themes in a context of approximate, suggestive and often provocative analogies with components of other works.

The most substantial texts linked to *Ulysses* in this manner are Homer's *Odyssey* and Shakespeare's *Hamlet*. That these texts play vital roles in Joyce's novel is well known, though the extent, variety and precision of the ironic relationships which Joyce sets up have not always been noticed. Other major authors hover about the perimeters of *Ulysses*, and many of Joyce's allusions to them operate ironically, as in the cases of Goethe and Yeats. This chapter, after noting one slight though engaging example of 'inter-authorial' irony, will concentrate largely on the ironic links between *Ulysses* and its two most assertively invoked forebears, the *Odyssey* and *Hamlet*.

An example of this kind of irony is furnished by the minor writer Mary Cecil Haye, whose name manifests itself only once in *Ulysses*, when it appears amid the thoughts of the minor character Miss Dunne, Blazes Boylan's secretary.

Although Miss Dunne is a marginal character about whom we hear few details, we do learn something of her tastes in fiction. She apparently prefers sentimental novels to more intellectual ones: in 'Wandering Rocks' she announces her plan to exchange Wilkie Collins' rather voyeuristic (though mostly undemanding) novel *The Woman in White* for 'another [novel] by Mary Cecil Haye' (10/372). *The Woman in White* has amusing affinities with what Miss Dunne would probably regard as the 'love-plot' of *Ulysses*, as she reminds us in a comment on Collins' text which becomes her one tentative venture into literary criticism: 'Too much mystery business in it. Is he in love with that one, Marion?' (10/371). ('Marion' is a name used by Molly Bloom, and Miss Dunne's comment seems a pointed if unconscious allusion to Molly, since the name is in fact spelt differently—as 'Marian'—in Collins' novel.) But what about Mary Cecil Haye?

Any sentimental writer might, no doubt, have served Joyce's purposes here. But a glance at the titles of works by Mary Cecil Haye suggests why he chose her in particular, for several of these titles also anticipate aspects or episodes of *Ulysses* as Miss Dunne might visualise them—perhaps especially if she had formulated a notion of the autobiographical functions of literature, akin to Stephen's view as expressed in his account of Shakespeare, and if she knew something of Joyce's life. Strikingly apposite titles of novels by Mary Cecil Haye include *A Shadow on the Threshold*; *The Sorrow of a Secret*; *A Wicked Girl*; *Victor and Vanquished*; *Hidden Perils*; *At the Seaside*; *For Her Dear Sake*; *Nora's Love Test*; and *Back to the Old Home*. It would not require great ingenuity to see these titles as forming an approximate summary—parodic and sometimes hyperbolic in a way Joyce especially enjoyed—of *Ulysses*.

Thus Joyce's inclusion of Mary Cecil Haye's name in the text of *Ulysses*, if he decided to incorporate it after considering the titles of her books, implies that the external world—as it appears in other people's writing—can furnish a gloss on the action of *Ulysses*; and also that the events shown in *Ulysses* could have been depicted in markedly different modes. It all depends on the angle from which we are looking.

Miss Dunne's interest in Mary Cecil Haye's novels reminds us, further, that many of the characters of *Ulysses* are, in their various ways, readers. Even Molly, despite her sometimes semi-literate conversation and her taste for pornography, shows an ability to respond with a modest degree of imaginative engagement to the literature she reads. (Molly's appetite for pornography, besides suggesting her boredom and her sense of sexual neglect, seems to balance Bloom's association with advertising, a form of propaganda—both pornography and propaganda being labelled 'kinetic' and improper art forms by the Stephen of the *Portrait*. Bloom, of course, has a certain interest in pornography as well.) In 'Calypso', Molly describes a novel to Bloom in terms which precisely anticipate Miss Dunne's report on *The Woman in White*, as well as alluding amusingly if unconsciously to *Ulysses* itself, its probable public reputation once published, and her own role in the plot as a woman briefly involved with a lover but finally still aligned with her husband: 'There's nothing smutty in it. Is she in love with the first fellow all the time?' (4/355-6).

The most substantial link between *Ulysses* and an antecedent text is its relationship to the *Odyssey*. Joyce stressed to early would-be readers of his novel that they should assimilate Homer's text before they embarked on *Ulysses*. On 14 October 1921, for example, he wrote to his aunt Josephine Murray: 'If you want to read *Ulysses* you had better first get or borrow from a library a translation in prose of the *Odyssey* of Homer' (*L I* 174). Joyce's debts to the *Odyssey* have been extensively catalogued elsewhere, notably by Gilbert, Ellmann (especially in *The Consciousness of Joyce*) and Michael Seidel. The question of the centrality and purpose of Joyce's use of Homeric material in *Ulysses* nevertheless remains vexed; but this question may have been deliberately devised by Joyce as a problem which no reader of his novel could solve. One reason why Joyce might have encouraged this doubt about his intentions is the degree of flexibility which it permits him in the use of irony. If a reader suspects on occasion that Joyce deploys Homer for important thematic value, and feels at other times that the Homeric material constitutes little more than structural scaffolding (and most readers do seem to oscillate between these two responses), Joyce thereby gains greater freedom to manipulate ironic parallels between his text and Homer's. His irony becomes more intricate in its operation, and more fluently bidirectional, through our uncertainty about its varying associations with meaning and with form. ('Fluently bidirectional' irony, in this context, allows Odysseus to qualify Bloom ironically, and Bloom to qualify Odysseus ironically, at the same time.)

That Joyce's deployment of Homeric material often becomes ironic in the sense developed in this study can hardly be questioned. The Homeric presence in *Ulysses* operates as an insistent focus for semantic disjunction, and constantly affects the implications of Joyce's text. Like irony itself, the Homeric material works on a wide range of scales, from minute to all-embracing, superficial to profound. Stephen's first spoken words in *Ulysses*—Tell me, Mulligan' (1/47)—recall a common opening phrase in epic but, in particular, precisely echo the opening of the *Odyssey* as rendered in the Butcher and Lang translation, which Joyce used: 'Tell me, Muse' (Homer/Butcher 1). At the other extreme, Joyce's Homeric schema provides an underlying structure massive enough to support the considerable weight of *Ulysses*.

Certain episodes of *Ulysses* seem especially saturated in Homeric details. 'Calypso' is rich in Homeric connotations, many of them ironical. We read, in the text of Milly's letter to her father, her condescending reference to farmers' wives through the slang phrase 'beef to the heels', an allusion to their plump ankles (4/403). The section of the *Odyssey* which focuses on Calypso contains an allusion to 'Ino of the fair

ankles' (Homer/Butcher 86). (The phrase may also be translated 'slim ankles', as by E. V. Rieu [Homer/Rieu 97].) Joyce
may well have had this passage in mind. The echo seems
slight, but it quietly calls attention to Joyce's sly manipulation
of the Homeric backdrop. Since 'Calypso' is the first episode
in which Bloom appears, Joyce probably felt that the Odyssean parallels needed especially detailed attention, both on
his own part and on that of his reader. In particular, he draws
on Homer to reinforce this episode's emphasis on the physical, which contrasts with the more ethereal tone of the three
preceding episodes focused on Stephen.

Another example of a strongly Homeric flavour is provided
by the 'Hades' episode, which incorporates allusions to the
four rivers of Hades and to Elpenor, analogue for the
deceased Patrick Dignam. As Gilbert remarks, 'this episode
has a number of other Homeric parallels, more easily recog-
nizable, nearer the surface, than the symbolic recalls in other
episodes. This comparative directness of allusion may be
ascribed to the near affinity of the ancient and modern
narratives, each of which records a visit to the abode of the
dead — the domain of Hades, Glasnevin cemetery' (Gilbert
167). The prevalence of Homeric parallels in 'Hades' also
suggests, as in the case of 'Calypso', Joyce's desire to
establish such patterns strongly within Bloom's first few
episodes. In the earlier 'Nestor' episode, Joyce's depiction of
his Nestor figure, Deasy the headmaster, must also be partly
based on an ironic inversion of the *Odyssey*. In Homer's text,
Athene advises Telemachus to 'go straight to Nestor, tamer of
horses: let us learn what counsel he hath in the secret of his
heart. And beseech him thyself that he may give unerring
answer; and he will not lie to thee, for he is very wise'
(Homer/Butcher 31). While Homer's Nestor can be a little
tedious in conversation, he seems to deserve the reputation
for veracity and wisdom which Athene here attributes to him.
Deasy contrasts strikingly with Nestor in these particular
respects. Though he causes Stephen no serious harm, and
though Stephen treats him with outward respect, Deasy

shows unmistakable signs of prejudice, misogyny and xenophobia; and he constantly dispenses historical fallacies and
ill-conceived advice.

Joyce's construction in *Ulysses* of a modern counterpart to
Homer's epic concentrates our attention, as it must have
concentrated Joyce's own attention, on matters like the
relationship of the classical and the modern, historical continuity and change, the very concept of equivalence, and in
particular, issues such as scale and perspective. As Seidel
points out, 'the very translated and reduced spaces of Dublin
provide a commentary, often parodic, on the larger and
longer movements of the Homeric original' (Seidel xi). But
this kind of 'miniaturising' process already occurs within the
Odyssey itself. Seidel observes that in describing Odysseus'
encounter with Aeolus, Homer 'miniaturizes the entire
Wanderings, as Odysseus sails for nine days only to have his
crew let the wind out of the bag on the tenth, blowing him
back just as he sights home' (Seidel 167). Joyce may have had
this existing Homeric practice in mind during his construction of the 'Wandering Rocks' episode, which performs a
similar function in showing readers of his novel how the
text's events and structures might appear if they were seen in
a different, much reduced scale. Senn shrewdly draws attention to an analogous case of Shakespearean 'miniaturising' in
Ulysses: he likens Master Patrick Dignam to Hamlet. 'Paddy
Dignam's dawdling is emphasized, an externalized counterpart of Prince Hamlet's hesitations. His father has recently
died, his mother is in mourning, and an uncle is in charge.
The uncle stages a little feast . . . from which Paddy absents
himself in disgust and boredom. The last glimpse of his father
was "on the landing", more or less in the way the dead king
makes his appearance on the stage' (Senn 194). (Another
possible literary source or inspiration for Joyce's meditations
on equivalence, scale and perspective suggests itself: Swift's
Gulliver's Travels.)

The *Odyssey* anticipates *Ulysses* in its incorporation of large
quantities of factual detail. For Homer, as for Joyce, a solid

factual stratum clearly seems a prerequisite for loftier and more ambitious material — whether that material be supernatural or symbolic. For example, Homer's careful provision of intricate instructions on boat-building, at moments when Odysseus needs to engage in that practice, makes more plausible those extravagant sections of the narrative which must have strained the credulity even of Homer's contemporary audience. Similarly, Joyce's earnest attention to the minutiae of Dublin geography permits the more bizarre portions of *Ulysses* — especially parts of its later episodes — to operate successfully on readers who might baulk at those extravagances if they were the first sections of the text to be encountered. (It is difficult to imagine ourselves confronting a novel which began with the 'Circe' or the 'Ithaca' episode, for example.) It may even be that both authors, Homer and Joyce, deliberately overstate their 'factual' material so that we will attend, with some sense of relief, to the more apparently odd or daring portions of their texts.

Thematically, the *Odyssey* anticipates *Ulysses* in several important respects. Its counterpointed strains of wandering and of longing for home are dominant strands in Joyce's novel as well. In *Ulysses* they appear with a less literal, more metaphorical emphasis than they possessed in Homer's text; but the theme of the possible clash between the desire and the ability to return home dominates extended portions of both works. Both texts draw attention to family relationships, domesticity, and household virtues. Odysseus, in his yearning for Ithaca, anticipates Bloom in his longing for a return to contentment at Eccles Street. Both texts, furthermore, stress the notion of timelessness and recurrence, the belief that everything which happens has occurred in the past in some form and will occur again, in still another guise, in the future. In its recapitulative relationship to the *Odyssey*, *Ulysses* also comes to embody this belief.

For both Homer and Joyce, the most appropriate human response to experience is usually acceptance and equanimity. These are emotional states which wise Odysseus, despite his trials (and his occasional violent outbursts), attains more readily than do other mortals in the text of Homer's poem (most of those around him tend to panic). Bloom achieves these emotions at the end of the novel as he calmly confronts the fact of Molly's infidelity, and throughout the day he behaves with more restraint and prudence than most of the other people we meet. Kenner lists some of Bloom's further attributes and endowments which associate him—approximately, and often parodically—with Odysseus: 'Stature, relative wealth, an exalted dwelling-place, handsome features, polysemous wit, a famously beautiful wife' (Kenner 1980: 44). Gilbert adds that, like Stephen, Bloom 'starts out from an *omphalos*, for, in the first scene of his Odyssey, entitled "Calypso", his home at No. 7 Eccles Street is . . . a replica, *mutatis mutandis*, of the isle of Ogygia, where Calypso dwelt; a "navel of the sea", as Homer calls it' (Gilbert 54).

One particular influence which may have encouraged Joyce to create more pointedly ironic links with Homer is his reading of Samuel Butler. Butler's *The Authoress of the Odyssey*, an engaging but rather perverse text, which remains largely unpersuasive for all Butler's energetic scholarly efforts, seeks to demonstrate that a woman—possibly the princess Nausicaa herself—wrote the *Odyssey*. Butler cites as evidence of female authorship the *Odyssey's* preoccupation with domestic values. (How a woman in Homer's society could have known so much about boat-building never becomes fully clear.) When Butler's critics pointed to the bloodshed in the *Odyssey* as a typically male preoccupation, he triumphantly replied that Homer at least made sure the blood was always cleaned up afterwards—an obvious sign of a woman's touch. Less quaintly, but still not quite convincingly, Butler claims that the *Odyssey's* sensitivity in treating human emotions and relationships would be beyond the capacity of a male author. Since the woman author's geographical knowledge scarcely extended beyond Sicily, Butler argues, nearly all the events of the *Odyssey* take place in settings whose details are demonstrably drawn from the topography of Sicily and its offshore islands. Subsequent scholars have mostly rejected Butler's conclusions— though a few of his claims, among numerous implausible ones, still seem provocative—but Joyce would have been untroubled by Butler's areas of academic vulnerability. More valuable to him would be the ironic charge imparted to Homer's text by Butler's iconoclastic manner of approaching it. His reading of Butler probably also suggested to Joyce that the *Odyssey* might be interpreted as a more personal, domestic, novelistic, psychological and even autobiographical document than it had usually been considered by previous readers.

Butler's two central assertions about the *Odyssey* both have striking affinities with Joyce's own interests, and may even have helped those interests to evolve. First, Butler's attempt to locate the *Odyssey* specifically in Sicily—partly by geographical analogy, partly by synecdoche, partly by arguments based on the specific knowledge possessed by the text's author—may have encouraged Joyce in his paradigmatic use of Dublin as a setting. If an island like Sicily can represent a larger realm, such as the entire Mediterranean, then so can a city like Dublin; and the city can represent the realm all the more comprehensively since it offers analogies of many kinds apart from the more purely topographical ones on which Butler concentrates in his discussion of the role played by Sicily in the *Odyssey*. Butler's claim that the famously wide-ranging voyages of Odysseus in fact confine themselves to the immediate environs of Sicily predicates for the *Odyssey* a kind and degree of irony seldom attributed to this text, though Butler himself does not use the term in such a way. This mode of Homeric irony resembles Joyce's own practices in *Ulysses*, where he uses irony both to associate Dublin with a larger realm and to manipulate parallels between his own characters and those of the *Odyssey*. Joyce's persistent use of this kind of synecdochic or metonymic irony—irony which operates by contrasting components in two different orders of geographical magnitude—recalls Butler's reading of the *Odyssey*.

Second, Butler's most striking claim, that the events of the *Odyssey* are narrated not from a magisterial external perspective (that of the traditionally endowed Homer) but from the viewpoint of a woman who may well have appeared in the text as a character, anticipates Joyce's own fondness for locating his narrative focus in unexpected places, for inserting obliquely autobiographical material into his fiction, and especially for visualising a typically 'male' environment from a 'female' point of view. Joyce constantly exploits the ironic disjunctions created by widely distributed or centrifugally contrasting narrative energies. Joyce's enthusiasm for this method certainly predates his writing of *Ulysses* (and presumably predates his reading of Butler). The method already contributes clearly to the treatment of Gabriel and Gretta Conroy in 'The Dead', for example. But Joyce employs this manner far more pervasively in *Ulysses* than he had ever done before. It may be that Butler's interpretation of the *Odyssey* encouraged Joyce's use of this mode.

It is even possible, as Ellmann has suggested, that Joyce's location of the narrative focus of the first half of the 'Nausicaa' episode within the consciousness of Gerty Mac-Dowell, the novel's Nausicaa figure, is a direct tribute to Butler and to his claim that Nausicaa wrote the *Odyssey*. Gerty, in a sense, contributes a section of narrative and an important new viewpoint: though Bloom is a stranger to her, she becomes (as we have seen) one of the few people in the novel to notice and respond to his unhappiness, an emotion which we regard as central to an understanding of Bloom's present circumstances. Also, the effect of Molly's monologue at the end of *Ulysses* — to show many of the novel's concerns from a radically different, feminine perspective and so to modify the impressions we have formed of them — recalls the transformation of our sense of the *Odyssey* which must occur if we take seriously Butler's radical assumptions about the work's authorship and point of view.

Butler argues, moreover, that Homer marks out Penelope as the vital female character in the *Odyssey*, and that other female characters in the poem seem merely variants of her. Circe and Calypso, in particular, are presented by Homer in this way. Joyce, similarly, envisages Molly as his novel's vital female character against whom all the others must be measured. Joyce's presentation of Molly may also owe something to Butler's claims about the historical evolution of the Penelope legend. According to Butler, in some pre-Homeric accounts Penelope had given herself indiscriminately to many of the suitors, and was consequently rejected by Odysseus on his return. Homer, in these terms, idealises the Penelope legend by stressing the character's fidelity. Joyce, analogously, presents Molly as the subject of veiled public speculation about her possible adulterous associations, and as the focus of Bloom's anxiety about cuckoldry, only to reveal through her monologue that Molly is almost as virtuous as Penelope, her single act of adultery being largely explicable in terms of her husband's persistent neglect of her. Further, Butler emphasises the self-contradictory nature of Homer's Penelope, and as we have seen, persistently self-contradictory impulses and statements characterise Molly as well.

Joyce also read Butler's essay called 'The Humour of Homer', which treats the *Iliad* as well as the *Odyssey*. Though less radical and provocative than *The Authoress of the Odyssey*, this study confirms Butler's penchant for iconoclastic and ironic readings. Here he suggests that the author of the *Iliad* may have been not a Greek at all but a Trojan, captured by the Greeks and compelled to compose poetry about Greek military successes. Butler ascribes to this Trojan Homer a remarkable capacity for using irony to subvert the onerous project, so that the whole *Iliad* becomes an ironic defence of the Trojan cause. (The fact, if it is a fact, that for thousands of years nobody else read the *Iliad* in this fashion would obviously trouble Butler not at all.) Butler also claims in this essay that the irony in Homer's writing is directed not at gods or women, but at men. These interpretations and emphases, especially the notion of reading part of Homer's work as a subversively ironical pro-Trojan text, must have appealed to Joyce, and may have further encouraged his own investigation of ironic modes. Butler, then, plays a significant role in *Ulysses* both through his own thoughts and interpretations and through the encouragement which he inadvertently gave to Joyce as he embarked on his quest for new, apposite and ironic readings of the *Odyssey*.

A further, more general source of irony in *Ulysses* may be Joyce's attention to the wide and sometimes self-contradictory range of Homeric scholarship. As Ellmann suggests in his discussion of this scholarship, 'Bérard and Butler treated the fabulous as factual; Bacon, with Vico after him, treated the factual as fabulous' (Ellmann 1977: 29). Joyce would feel no obligation to choose between these divergent emphases, and may even have found them salutary as he manipulated parallels between Homer's text and his own. Throughout *Ulysses*, in any case, Joyce makes frequent use of the possible reciprocity, even the occasional identity, of the 'fabulous' and the 'factual'.

In writing *Ulysses*, Joyce alludes to Shakespeare, the author he most admired and envied, almost as extensively as he draws on Homer. In a letter to Ezra Pound, Joyce refers to the 'Scylla and Charybdis' episode as 'the Hamlet chapter' (*L I* 101). He seems to have envisaged a kind of triangular linkage among the *Odyssey*, *Hamlet* and *Ulysses*, and to have bolstered it by considering analogies between Homer's text and Shakespeare's. As Ellmann points out, each of Joyce's predecessors presents a character (Orestes, Hamlet) who appears as a 'prince avenging a royal father's murder by an adulterer' (Ellmann 1977: 45). Telemachus and Hamlet must both deal with usurpers. Gertrude's notorious infidelity might be contrasted with Penelope's famous fidelity. Mahaffey comments: 'The insight that the *Odyssey* expresses in spatial terms as the necessity of circumspection and circumnavigation, *Hamlet*, the other major precursor of *Ulysses*, explores in terms of heredity: straightforward movement is equally impossible through space *and* time' (Mahaffey 193). Speculations about such topics probably encouraged Joyce to develop the intricately ironic associations which he sets up between his novel and its two chief antecedents.

Joyce's invocations and applications of Shakespeare appear less fundamental and 'structural' than his Homeric borrowings, yet they seem to be more diverse among themselves; and they differ crucially from the Homeric borrowings in that several characters in *Ulysses* notice analogies between their own circumstances and the situations depicted in Shakespeare's texts—a kind of conscious perception of affinities which is aroused nowhere in *Ulysses* by the Homeric material. Besides considering such perceptions, however, we must also investigate those ironic associations with Shakespeare (especially those involving *Hamlet*) which do operate in a similar way to the Homeric associations—essentially, in remaining undetected by the novel's characters.

Joyce bases the broad episodic structure of *Ulysses* chiefly on that of the *Odyssey*, and structural analogies with Shakespeare are more difficult to detect. Nevertheless, the opening scene of 'Telemachus' recalls the opening scene of *Hamlet* in various ways, so alerting us to watch for such analogies wherever they do appear in the novel. The tower-top at Sandycove echoes the battlements at Elsinore, and Stephen's black clothing and dour mood recall attributes of Hamlet, as the 'gay attire' and flippant demeanour of Mulligan and Haines evoke Rosencrantz and Guildenstern. As Kenner points out, Mulligan also echoes Claudius in several respects (Kenner 1956: 194). Stephen seems isolated, embattled, and trapped in melancholy; and he frets about the recent death of a parent, feeling that he is haunted by the parent's ghost—a sensation which becomes almost literal in the 'Circe' episode. Stephen also finds evidence of insensitivity, betrayal and usurpation everywhere he looks. The worldly people who surround him, like Mulligan and Deasy, urge him to adopt a facile cheerfulness, and they do so more to ease their own situations (which are unsettled by Stephen's persistent brooding) than out of real concern for his unhappiness, an unhappiness which in any event they mock or profess not to understand. In all these ways, of course, Stephen's position closely resembles that of Hamlet. Such analogies seem less pronounced in subsequent episodes of *Ulysses*, except perhaps in 'Proteus', which resembles a soliloquy uttered by Stephen; many of the analogies have been discussed by critics, notably by William M. Schutte in *Joyce and Shakespeare* and by Ellmann in *The Consciousness of Joyce*.

So insistent do the Shakespearean associations in the novel often appear, indeed, that minor and imperceptive characters occasionally detect them. The opening scene of *Ulysses* becomes so markedly Shakespearean that even Haines (who in the grandiose and intellectually charged context of 'Telemachus' could hardly seem more insignificant, or more obtuse) perceives analogies between the present setting and that of *Hamlet*: 'I mean to say . . . this tower and these cliffs here remind me somehow of Elsinore. *That beetles o'er his base into the sea*, isn't it?' (1/566-8). Mulligan, like Haines, has in part been prompted to such insights by Stephen's formulation of a 'Shakespeare theory' which concentrates on *Hamlet*, and by Stephen's deliberate Hamlet mannerisms; yet he too detects Shakespearean analogues for present events which go beyond those parallels that Stephen knowingly or unknowingly evokes for him.

Bloom's approach to literature seems engagingly pragmatic, and we hear in particular that he has 'applied to the works of William Shakespeare more than once for the solution of difficult problems in imaginary or real life' (17/385-7). Despite these earnest investigations, his knowledge of the content of the plays probably remains rudimentary. Yet Bloom's thoughts contain numerous allusions to Shakespeare: Schutte counts 47, including 28 to *Hamlet* (Schutte 124). Bloom's consciousness, then, contributes quite significantly to the

Shakespearean stratum and flavour of *Ulysses*. Like Joyce, Bloom shows some awareness of a succession of wry analogies between present circumstances and Shakespearean precedents; most of his Shakespearean 'allusions' constitute ironic glosses, informed by more or less accurate quotations from the plays, on his actual situation.

The most important forum for Shakespearean awareness in *Ulysses*, of course, remains Stephen's consciousness. In his library seminar he focuses with some skill on the deliberate perceptions of Shakespeare achieved by various characters in the novel. The discussion achieves far more importance as an imaginative component of Joyce's text than it could ever possess as a contribution by Stephen to literary history or criticism. Though often labelled a 'Shakespeare theory', the material Stephen presents pays only erratic attention to historical evidence about the biography of Shakespeare, and scarcely constitutes a theory. In fact, as Seidel provocatively points out, Stephen's iconoclastic treatment of Shakespeare closely resembles Butler's treatment of Homer (Seidel 84). Rather, Stephen's talk operates as Joyce's most daring attempt to allow a character within one of his texts to manipulate an elaborate ironic parallel which also becomes structurally important to that text itself. The discussion, furthermore, helps Stephen to define his conception of the artist's role in literary Dublin. The Shakespeare he presents, identified by Stephen with Hamlet's father, is bold and resolute, a repudiation of the tendency of the librarians (and others) to identify Shakespeare with the apparently vacillating, indecisive Prince Hamlet. Stephen may mean partly that he should model himself on this quality in the senior Hamlet, and overcome his tendency to emulate its negative counterpart in the junior one.

Many readers have noticed how closely Bloom resembles the Shakespeare described by Stephen: 'a restless man with a lively daughter and a dead son, uneasily yoked to a wife who "overbore" him once and cuckolds him now' (Kenner 1980: 114). Bloom's frequent use of Shakespearean phrases, and even his possession of a rudimentary 'Shakespeare theory' of his own (5/196-7), may serve to make the association more plausible for us. But Joyce simultaneously and systematically undermines such associations, thus ensuring that they remain problematic. Bloom, though urbane and moderately cultured, with 'a touch of the artist' about him (10/582), is scarcely a literary figure of Shakespearean proportions. Joyce also takes some trouble to differentiate Bloom from Hamlet's father, as if to cast oblique doubt on Stephen's rather glib (if provocative) association of Shakespeare with this dramatic character. We recall Hamlet's father as a spectacular ghost, making his bold first appearance on a high platform, and urging revenge. Bloom, by contrast, first appears to us quietly preparing breakfast for his wife in a basement kitchen; far from seeming to be a ghost, he is emphatically described in physical terms through the mention of his fondness for such delicacies as 'the inner organs of beasts and fowls' (4/1-2); and when he later offers advice, notably to Stephen in 'Eumaeus' or to the pub patrons in 'Cyclops', he usually seeks to dissuade his listeners from vengeful behaviour, and to recommend conciliation.

Bloom himself seldom manages to act decisively: in the context of his marital problems he seems to postpone analysis and resolution, as Hamlet does when considering his own difficulties. Thus the Shakespeare discussion in *Ulysses* works in intricately ironic ways, especially when we associate it with Bloom. It is ironic, as readers often note, that Stephen invokes with seeming admiration a Shakespeare who resembles the central character in *Ulysses*, but then pays scant attention to that character when he meets him in the flesh — fleetingly within 'Scylla and Charybdis' itself and more extensively in the episodes from 'Oxen of the Sun' to 'Ithaca'. The irony is complicated, however, by Bloom's imperfect resemblances to Shakespeare and his striking divergence from Hamlet's father, since many of Stephen's hypotheses rest on the assumption that Shakespeare projected his own personality onto this character. This web of irony serves to ensure a problematic basis for Stephen's discussion, and to prevent its meshing too neatly with its context in *Ulysses*, but also to enhance its provocative aspects.

Ironic associations between *Ulysses* and texts by other writers, as discussed in this chapter, might seem to challenge Joyce's powers of literary control more assertively than associations with texts already written by himself. Especially in the cases of the *Odyssey* and *Hamlet*, the existing works possess their own formal structure and textual authority, which might appear to limit their usefulness to Joyce. He could more readily bend to his purposes a text like the *Portrait*, a few aspects of which, indeed, he may even have crafted with their future role as ironic antecedents to *Ulysses* consciously in his mind: during 1914 and 1915 he was working on both novels.

Yet Joyce's ironic application of Homer and Shakespeare unfolds so deftly that such considerations become immaterial. While his respect for these authors remains genuine, he is unencumbered by antiquarian esteem for their textual inviolability, and he adapts them to his own uses with considerable energy. Nor does he employ the ironic associations for the chief purpose of limiting or ridiculing the characters and scenes depicted in his novel's present, as T. S. Eliot might have done. Irony operates bidirectionally here, just as it does in the case of affinities with Joyce's other works, or in the case of associations within the text of *Ulysses* itself. The magnitude of Hamlet's difficulties may highlight Stephen's exaggerated or self-indulgent responses to his own problems; or Odysseus' enterprise, decisiveness and courage may qualify Bloom's more limited practical capabilities and show him as ineffectual. But, perhaps more importantly, Stephen's avoidance of violent responses suggests that, in the end, it is Hamlet who over-reacts to his circumstances, while Bloom's modesty and gentleness qualify the bravado and occasional belligerence of Odysseus. This bidirectional irony qualifies a distinction which Kenner draws between *Ulysses* and *Finnegans Wake*: '*Finnegans Wake* may differ from

Ulysses chiefly in this, that whereas in the earlier book Bloom occupies the foreground, re-enacting unawares Odysseus' adventures, in the later book's universe it would be just as pertinent to say that Odysseus was enacting the adventures of Bloom' (Kenner 1983: 230). In terms of the present analysis, the claim that Odysseus can 'enact' Bloom's adventures applies to the universe of *Ulysses* as well as to that of the *Wake*.

The most obvious common ground shared by Bloom and Stephen as they contrast ironically with Odysseus and Hamlet is their preference for non-violent solutions. Joyce seemingly thought, perhaps too optimistically, that twentieth-century society could resolve its difficulties without recourse to the violent and vengeful modes of behaviour—summarised by Stephen, in a Shakespearean phrase, as a 'bloodboltered shambles' (9/133-4)—recounted in much classical and Renaissance literature.

Further, Joyce's ironic superimposition of Homeric and Shakespearean modes onto the Dublin of 1904 and the literary consciousness of the early twentieth century emphasises the diversity, but also the ironic intermeshings and synonymities, of various myths and explanations of life. Though the classical and Renaissance periods appear so different from the modern era, Joyce's reliance on their literary methods stresses those affinities which they do possess—with the present day and also, by analogy, with one another. And since Homer and Shakespeare also synthesised earlier modes of expression and (certainly in Shakespeare's case, and probably in Homer's) permitted previously incompatible literary elements to coexist and jostle in their texts, they had in fact already employed a type of ironic technique which closely anticipates Joyce's own manner. Joyce's ironic deployment of Homeric and Shakespearean parallels, then, also serves to show his awareness of this path on which both authors had preceded him.

Moreover, both the *Odyssey* and *Hamlet* are works with intricate histories of their own. That of the *Odyssey* is more

obscure, but according to Joyce's chosen source Victor Bérard, Homer's text draws on various earlier accounts of the
adventures of Odysseus. Certainly, it had already become a
kind of composite work by the time of Virgil, who fused it
with the *Iliad* and *Argonautica*. Countless subsequent authors
proceeded to make use of Homer. Joyce shows awareness of
several of these authors in *Ulysses*; and he joins them by
adding further layers and complexities to the historical
matrix. *Hamlet* as fashioned by Shakespeare is also a composite work, dependent on a motley variety of literary ances-
tors, and hence, implicitly, it functions as a commentary on
the links which may be found or forged between different
literary traditions. It has, of course, been invoked by numerous authors for various purposes, and again Joyce exploits
this phenomenon—the role of *Hamlet* in establishing a tradition of references to itself—within *Ulysses*, as well as
contributing new elements to the tradition. In using the
Odyssey and *Hamlet* in *Ulysses*, Joyce draws on an oral text
compiled and recited at the outset of the Western literary
tradition and a dramatic text written and performed at an
intermediate high point in that tradition, in the course of
creating a third work which may occupy a comparable
eminence in the modern era, and which is highly self-
conscious about its own identity as a printed book. He also
bridges or fuses an epic poem and a play in the process of
fashioning a novel.

It seems likely, furthermore, that Joyce envisaged the
Odyssey and *Hamlet* as embodying and articulating two distinct psychological orientations or modes of thought, each
particularly representative of the historical period of the work
in question but also suggestive of perennial human impulses.
The characters in *Ulysses* appear in their turn to oscillate, and
sometimes to choose, between the same two modes, as if to
remind us that the modes are indeed perennial but also to
suggest that in the modern era both necessarily coexist. If
Hamlet represents the height of Renaissance self-consciousness, the *Odyssey* seems to a modern reader strikingly lacking

in self-consciousness, and between these two extremes Joyce's characters frequently have to steer. In terms of *Ulysses*, the opposition accords precisely with Stephen's obviously keen knowledge that he plays the role of Hamlet and his seemingly complete ignorance that he plays the role of Telemachus. The opposition also finds a faint echo or parody in the contrast between Bloom's relative knowledge of Shakespeare and his apparent ignorance of Homer—even though he regards his pragmatic, fact-hunting reading of Shakespeare as largely fruitless, and even though we can readily imagine him enjoying the *Odyssey* if he were to read it. Joyce has been careful to include in *Ulysses* no hint that Bloom knows the *Odyssey*; but we must be tempted to wonder whether, if he did know it, he would perceive any analogies—even ironic ones—between Odysseus' circumstances and his own.

7

Ironies of the Real World

As we move from the most immediate and local ironies of *Ulysses* to its largest and most wide-ranging ones, we find it increasingly difficult to achieve semantic certainty, to know whether what seems to be there on the page is present in fact. Current scepticism about the wisdom and value of intuiting authorial intentions allows us some degree of detachment from this problem, though any study of ironic modes will sometimes wish to challenge that scepticism in its turn: we must often feel tempted to consider whether a particular case of irony is 'deliberate' or not. Booth's convincing account of ironic operations depends on an assumption that authorial intent requires critical scrutiny in any assessment of such operations. This issue of intention will be investigated more fully in the eighth chapter.

As we complete our quest for ironic locations exploited in *Ulysses*, moreover, we must leave behind not only texts written by Joyce himself but texts of all kinds. In these realms we clearly need to proceed with considerable circumspection. Many enticing assumptions about Joyce's ironic use of the 'real world'—the world outside texts, the world which was there all the time without him, in the form of hard facts rather than literary transcriptions—have to be set aside for lack of evidence. Only instances founded in particularly well-documented 'facts', and of obvious purpose within *Ulysses*, will be considered in any detail here. The term 'irony', moreover, becomes progressively vaguer in its implications once we move beyond texts, as Booth has emphasised (Booth 2); when we allow ourselves to discuss concepts like 'the irony of circumstances', the word potentially approaches the futile status of denoting virtually everything. In an attempt to

avoid such problems of definition, this chapter will concentrate largely on cases which contain a particularly obvious
and vital verbal component in the external environment as
well as in the textual one: for example, those which focus on
place names, accounts of topography, historical narratives or
autobiographical analogies.

We might ponder why Joyce made such wide use of
external ironies in *Ulysses*. One of the more immediate and
straightforward explanations may relate to his deployment of
Homer. The *Odyssey*, however we conceive of its authorship
and other crucial circumstances, undoubtedly exploits geography for insistent and often ironic purposes; indeed, it
probably makes more pervasively ironic use of geography
than any other text composed before *Ulysses*. In taking the
Odyssey as a model and analogue, Joyce clearly noted and
emulated this aspect of Homer's text. His contemplation
of analogies between Odysseus' wanderings in the Mediterranean and Bloom's wanderings in Dublin, moreover,
inevitably led Joyce to consider slippery associations of
geographical fact which, transferred to a text which plays
with those analogies, necessarily become ironical.

Ironies of the real world may involve history as well as
geography: again, Joyce's interest in Homer, and in Shakespeare as well, encourages him into ironic juxtapositions
involving different times as well as different places. Joyce
recognises the further irony that differing views of the same
historical data may create division and uncertainty. In
extreme cases the contemplation of history generates 'night-
mare', as Stephen says to Mr Deasy (2/377). Moreover,
Joyce's oblique eye for autobiographical analogies leads him
to accommodate in his text meditations on possible ironic
relationships between the circumstances of his characters and
those of his own life. Here we encounter the phenomenon
which Ellmann has aptly designated the blurred margin: in
other words, some of Joyce's autobiographical allusions and
ironies shade into realms which we can never fully comprehend because he deliberately kept pieces of vital information

to himself. One of the definitive ironies of *Ulysses*, then, is that in certain parts of the novel we cannot know enough about the text's implications even to be sure whether it operates ironically or not.

As we consider the range of external locations which Joyce invokes for ironic purposes in *Ulysses*, there might seem to be an irreconcilable division between clearly apposite literary texts (like *Dubliners*, the *Portrait*, the *Odyssey*, or *Hamlet*) and apparently random, extra-literary facets of the 'real world'. Written texts, while we may often debate the methods and details of their interpretation, seem relatively free of problems at least in terms of their physical characteristics. Though Joyce made considerable efforts (not always successfully) to ensure that his own works were published in the precise form he wished, he never seems to have felt much bibliographical anxiety about the texts of the past. *Hamlet*, and especially the *Odyssey*, pose serious problems of textual reliability, but Joyce never paid particular attention to such problems: he simply used chosen editions of these works, for all they were worth and for his own purposes. By contrast, the external world beyond literary texts creates considerable difficulties for those people (such as geographers, historians and biographers) who seek to determine its exact contours and the precise modes of change which it undergoes.

Nevertheless, if Joyce's ironic references to the real world mostly operate in a similar fashion to his ironic literary allusions, and this study argues that they do, then we need to consider what mechanisms permit such a metaphysical parallel to be sustained. Two such mechanisms appear to work, in an almost reciprocal manner, in Ulysses.

First, Joyce ensures that *Ulysses* incorporates vast quantities of plausible 'factual' detail concerning people, events, times and, especially, places. Much of this detail derives from demonstrably 'historical' sources. For all the necessarily controversial nature of the process of recalling and recording the past, many facets of the historical matrix presented in *Ulysses* would be accepted by qualified observers as an essentially authentic account of life in Dublin in 1904. Thus a solid naturalistic structure underlies the whole novel. This structure undergoes considerable buffeting from stylistic extravagances in the later episodes, and is subjected throughout the text to Joyce's probing scepticism, but these forces only serve to stress its inevitable presence and resilience. *Ulysses* thus pays tribute to the irreducible physical reality of the external world, both philosophically and through the incorporation of innumerable minute details drawn from actuality. This process ensures that the novel's explicit references to that external world will operate smoothly and convincingly whenever their context requires them to do so.

Such a literary method also acknowledges a world that existed before the novel and exists beyond it, a realm with its own intricate structure and interconnections which the novel adduces only partially and in passing. As Kenner remarks, 'though the city in the book is a city of words, it corresponds so minutely to a city in Ireland that facts drawn from that city dovetail into the book even when the book does not mention them' (Kenner 1983: 228). The success of *Ulysses* in evoking a plausible (and demonstrably precise) sense of geographical and historical authenticity has seldom been questioned, even by readers who feel troubled by other dimensions of the novel. By constructing *Ulysses* in this way, Joyce ensures that we will accept the novel's judgments of the external world as readily as (and in essentially the same way that) we accept its judgments of other texts. He also deploys his factual data to show how the real world may outdistance human observations of it. As Kenner has observed, Joyce recognised that Naturalism is 'an essentially ambivalent convention. It parades an ironic obsession with what the characters see in order to express what they ignore. It affords the artist immersed in a provincial society leverage for exhibiting the condition of man' (Kenner 1956: 76).

Second, Joyce shows considerable skill in treating the external world, where necessary, as if it was itself a text. Once assimilated into the highly verbal environment of

Ulysses, that world will necessarily take on some textual attributes; but Joyce demonstrates a remarkable gift for imagining that such a conversion into text occurs even before this inevitable assimilation takes place. Verbal aspects of phenomena—their names, descriptions of their status or arguments about it—receive especially close attention throughout *Ulysses*. Thus the real world invoked in *Ulysses* attains its own prior textual quality, and so appears as a succession or collection of texts. This emphasis, again, helps us to see Joyce's allusions to literary texts and to facets of the actual world as forming a continuum.

Such a process of conversion to text operates with particular facility in the case of historical data. We most often recall such data in the form of other witnesses' verbal accounts, since we ourselves have not usually been present when particular events occurred: that is, we cannot coherently confine our sense of history to knowledge of those incidents which we have personally witnessed. History thus transforms itself readily into verbal recapitulation and anecdote: our awareness of developments in time tends, with fluctuating degrees of fidelity to historical facts, to take textual form. In situations where observers disagree radically about the course of events—recent Irish history is obviously a case in point—various texts will often jostle for acceptance.

Joyce exploits this phenomenon for ironic effect in the 'Nestor' episode, where Deasy relies on questionable and sometimes erroneous narratives (cherished like the shells in his collection) to vindicate his view of history. As Adams points out, 'though Mr Deasy goes straight to the point, he is always wrong' (Adams 20). Deasy claims, for example, that Sir John Blackwood 'voted for the union' (2/279), but in fact Blackwood opposed the Act of Union, and 'he never rode to Dublin to vote for or against it, because he died in the act of putting on his topboots in order to go vote against it' (Adams 20). The misogynistic Deasy also skews or reverses historical facts in compiling the stories which he delights in telling to blame women for the downfall of Irish leaders. Finally, 'to cap the climax of his historical absurdities, Mr Deasy is made to say that "the orange lodges agitated for repeal of the union twenty years before O'Connell did". This is simple madness. . . . The Orange lodges were pro-Union and could not rationally have been anything else' (Adams 22). But it is easier to demonstrate that Deasy is wrong than to furnish an alternative account of events which would, in turn, convince all observers of its own reliability. Thus conflicting narratives inevitably compose the web of recorded history, and Joyce exploits this pattern to help locate his novel, as a work of 'fiction', in a world of 'facts' which at times seems scarcely more fixed or substantial than the novel itself.

Joyce probably believed that all recorded history worked in this ironic fashion, through its juxtaposition of accounts of the past which are mutually contradictory yet endorsed by their respective adherents as unassailable truth. In *Ulysses*, as in his other writings, he naturally concentrates on Irish history, as a concern in itself, as a context for his particular characters, and as a microcosm or paradigm of the history of the world. In the earliest episodes of *Ulysses* he displays a keen awareness of the ironic disjunctions which the recording of history seems to propagate. As John Henry Raleigh remarks in his essay, '*Ulysses*: Trinitarian and Catholic', 'in the Telemachiad what Joyce has done with "the Irish question" is to place a dull Saxon, batty to boot, between two brilliant Celts. As a final irony, it is only the Englishman who is a student of Gaelic and a supporter of the Gaelic League' (Newman and Thornton 107). (The Englishman Haines remains, incidentally, the only Gaelic speaker anywhere in the novel.) In his essay on James Clarence Mangan, Joyce had already drawn attention to a certain kind of historical irony which, he claims, Ireland demonstrates with particular frequency, but which can be assumed to operate elsewhere. He notes that the popularity of political leaders seldom guarantees either the longevity of their reputations or the achievement of lasting harmony among their devotees: 'In Ireland, a country destined by God to be the eternal caricature of the serious world, even when the monuments are for the most popular men, whose character is most amenable to the will of the people, they rarely get beyond the laying of the foundation stone' (*CW* 176).

Joyce's own portrayal of Irish history may, at times, have demonstrated some of the ironic ambivalence which he attributes to his compatriots. Ellsworth Mason and Richard Ellmann observe in their Introduction to Joyce's *Critical Writings*: 'Never more Irish than when he attacks his country, after parading Irish history as a succession of betrayals, [Joyce] cannot help invoking its special beauty and worth in the face of English oppression' (*CW* 9). Adams adds: 'Joyce intended to suggest that the history of his country, like its language, was the diversion of well-mannered, well-spoken, but essentially cold and selfish usurpers' (Adams 32).

The conversion of external reality into text may seem more difficult in the case of geographical data. People readily derive such data from sense impressions, especially visual ones; all readers of *Ulysses*, even those with no direct experience of Dublin, will visualise the novel's settings on the basis of personal experience, usually experience of scenes in some way similar to those shown by Joyce, perhaps occasionally of contrasting ones. Joyce may, himself, have been influenced in this manner by his experience of cities other than Dublin; we need to remind ourselves that he never visited Ireland during the years when *Ulysses* was being written. People usually supplement their direct experience of geographical facts with recorded information, most frequently in the shape of maps; Joyce has an obvious fascination with such documents and with the conceptions of place which they encourage people to form. Though he would scarcely have needed to see maps of Dublin in order to write *Ulysses*, he used them extensively, and much evidence (as in his correspondence with friends and relatives who still lived in Dublin) testifies to his persistent quest for maps, plans, timetables and similar documentary material to consult as he constructed the novel. Joyce certainly required maps in order to evoke Molly's recollections of Gibraltar, a place which he had never visited. In 'Wandering Rocks', an episode which makes extremely detailed use of the textures of the urban environment, geography appears to be regarded in a cartographic almost as much as in a verbal manner. 'Ithaca', likewise, explores other modes of measurement besides verbal ones, and thus seems able to invoke geographical concepts in more intricate ways than we might expect to find in a novel.

Yet the study of geography, like that of history, also has its own intrinsically verbal and textual dimension, and Joyce exploits this aspect fully. Verbal accounts of places which we have not visited, or of places which have now changed from an earlier state, may become our only means of access to certain settings, just as similar accounts may form our only path to some types of historical knowledge. Descriptions of particular places may invest them with characteristics which we would not ourselves detect there if we visited, as we realise frequently when we read the *Odyssey*. In *Ulysses* Joyce plays with the ways in which people respond to verbal descriptions of place, usually by depicting Bloom's reactions to accounts of this kind, such as his copious meditation inspired by the 'Agendath Netaim' advertisement which he reads in 'Calypso' (4/154-239).

In his ironic deployment of geography in *Ulysses*, Joyce seemingly expects from his readers a familiarity with the urban landscape of Dublin resembling the detailed knowledge of texts which his novel demonstrably requires. We need to recognise that his cartographic appropriations and distortions work in essentially the same manner as his literary ones. For readers lacking access to Dublin, and even for inhabitants of the actual city as it undergoes historical change and progressively ceases to resemble the Dublin of 1904, the requisite knowledge is problematic in a way that knowledge of texts is not. Yet Joyce treats these two kinds of knowledge similarly, with the obvious implication that his readers should manage to acquire them both, even in difficult circumstances.

As Hart points out, when the Viceroy crosses the Grand Canal in the 'Wandering Rocks' episode, the name 'Royal Canal' is bestowed on it (Hart and Hayman 199). The Royal Canal is, in reality, on the opposite side of Dublin, and Joyce clearly transfers the name purposively in order to emphasise the Viceroy's character and habits, his (lofty and pretentious, if partly unconscious) attribution of 'royal' status to all the objects and circumstances which surround him. The successful operation of this irony depends on a reader's knowledge that the canal crossed by the Viceroy was never known as 'Royal' until Joyce allocated that name to it; and the irony becomes stronger when we discover that the real Royal Canal exists on the other side of Dublin. (On a map, in fact, the Grand and Royal Canals approach a mirror-symmetrical configuration which makes Joyce's transposition of their names seem particularly neat.)

A subtler geographical irony occurs in the eleventh section of 'Wandering Rocks'. Here Dilly Dedalus attempts, with little success, to prompt her father Simon to behave like a responsible provider to his family, while he would prefer to remain an unencumbered bon vivant and drinking companion to his friends. It seems ironically appropriate, in these terms, that their encounter should take place in a street called Bachelor's Walk: Simon behaves more like a bachelor than the family man his daughter thinks he should resemble, and twice attempts to evade Dilly by walking away from her. Joyce does not specify the street name anywhere in the text, and the irony thus requires local knowledge, or study, to unearth. Yet the ironic aptness of the setting is striking, and can scarcely be accidental. Adams points out a similar geographical irony: 'When Simon Dedalus has just finished haggling over pennies with his hungry and shabby daughter Dilly, he passes a shop known in the novel as Reddy and Daughter's. . . . The addition [to a real name] of "and

Daughter's", an ironic parallel to the usual "& Sons" as well as a possible but mythical partner, draws an emphatic line beneath Simon's unfatherly attitudes' (Adams 88).

In 'Telemachus', Stephen and Mulligan look from the Martello tower 'towards the blunt cape of Bray Head that lay on the water like the snout of a sleeping whale' (1/181-2). Bray Head does indeed look very like a whale, but is completely invisible from the tower at Sandycove, being concealed by intervening land. This initially puzzling reference, unlikely to be a mistake by the factually fastidious Joyce, may serve as an early warning to the reader (five pages into the novel's text) to take nothing for granted. Read with pedantic attention, after all, the sentence never claims explicitly that Stephen and Mulligan can see Bray Head at the present moment; they may well be looking towards it, having their view blocked by that intervening land, and recalling the Head's demeanour from their previous experience. The image of Bray Head, and the whale simile, seem in any case to occupy Stephen's thoughts more than Mulligan's. We know from the *Portrait* that Stephen had lived at Bray as a child; and Stephen's myopia, possibly accentuated by a recent accident to his glasses (recalling a similar accident which had occurred during his schooldays), would prevent his seeing Bray clearly even if it were visible from the tower. The whale reference recalls remarks made by Polonius in *Hamlet*, and so links itself obliquely to Stephen's interest in Shakespeare. All these apposite connotations are quietly invoked by Joyce's geographical irony. The allusion to the invisible Bray Head as if it were visible also finds a remarkably precise echo at the other end of the novel: in 'Penelope', Molly recalls looking from Gibraltar towards 'the bay of Tangier white and the Atlas mountain with snow on it' (18/859-60). But to an observer in Gibraltar Tangiers is concealed by intervening land (like Bray Head from the tower), and the Atlas range, as Joyce must have known, is over the horizon.

Ulysses also incorporates numerous autobiographical references and hints operating in an ironic manner. These elements, intriguingly, have clear affinities with the historical and geographical components which also work ironically. Semantic and formal discrepancies, which informed readers will notice, signal the presence of all these types of irony.

Joyce bestows on Stephen Dedalus various aspects of, and incidents derived from, his own circumstances in mid-1904: for example, life in the Martello tower at Sandycove with a witty, oppressive medical student and a slightly demented Englishman; the rather difficult enunciation to a sceptical audience of an idiosyncratic view of Shakespeare and of literature; and a rescue by a philanthropic passerby after a violent, unwanted (but partly self-provoked) physical encounter in a street. Any of these personal attributions, from author to character, might plausibly have operated in the confessional, apologetic or retributive fashion which autobiography often assumes—especially since they all show Stephen (or Joyce) in a state of precise moral equilibrium: as a victim, but also as a person bearing a largely unacknowledged responsibility for the oppression he suffers. Yet Joyce deftly qualifies and revalues all these detailed links by the simple strategy of choosing for *Ulysses* the particular date on which its events occur. It is clear that 16 June 1904 marked for Joyce a crucial stage in his relationship with Nora Barnacle, whatever precisely occurred on that date (and part of the point is that we can never know for certain what it was, though we might suspect a sexual encounter of some kind). To choose this date for *Ulysses* was, for Joyce, a deliberately private act of commemoration. It was also an act of differentiation: a way to distinguish himself from Stephen Dedalus. Whatever significant transaction occurred between Joyce and Nora on that day, we can be certain that nothing of the kind happens in the life of Stephen, whose most characteristic modes of behaviour in *Ulysses* correlate with his solitude.

The juxtaposition of Stephen and Bloom, as is well known, has its own autobiographical resonances. Bloom's age, a few of his traits of personality, and several central characteristics of his wife, are recognisably drawn from Joyce's life and family circumstances at the time he was writing *Ulysses*. It is as if Bloom has experienced the encounter with Nora which took place for Joyce on 16 June 1904, a meeting which has been denied to Stephen. Bloom may embody those aspects of Joyce which the encounter particularly evoked or called into being. The meeting of Stephen and Bloom wryly demonstrates Joyce's acceptance of the limitations of his own earlier life, when he had resembled Stephen in many ways, but also the limitations of his present life, when he more closely resembles Bloom. Yet Joyce clearly shared the sense which most readers acquire that Bloom is the superior character in his equanimity, capacity for acceptance and power of restraint, and thus represents an advance on Stephen's position. The meeting of Stephen and Bloom brings into play numerous semantic disjunctions, many of them mentioned (earlier in this book and elsewhere) in accounts of the 'Ithaca' episode, and most of them involving irony. The temporary alignment of the characters Stephen and Bloom, indeed, rather resembles the operation of a verbal irony, in its invocation of misunderstandings and alternative interpretations of similar data inspected from two points of view.

Joyce's attempts to draw a parallel between his allusions to texts and his allusions to the 'real world', the world of experience, have thematic implications involving the relationship of text and world. Texts other than *Ulysses*, and the factual world outside *Ulysses*, appear to occupy essentially the same spiritual space once allusions to them have been activated within the bounds of the novel; and an important part of the novel's quest, indeed, is to secure this kind of alignment. Joyce deploys similar types of irony in dealing with both realms, a practice which further reinforces the process of seeking or creating parallels. One of Joyce's implications is that once texts have been published, they enter the realm of historical fact. Since in *Ulysses* he treats *Dubliners*, *Exiles* and especially the *Portrait* as texts, much as he treats the *Odyssey* and *Hamlet*, he emphasises further that this pattern applies to his own works as well as to those composed by other writers. A further implication, inevitably, is that a similar process will some day operate in the case of *Ulysses* itself.

Joyce's use of 'external' ironies also helps to convey the theme that real world and text, 'fact' and 'fiction', mingle indissolubly. His epistemological concern draws on humble models, such as data about Dublin to be found in *Thom's Directory*, from which he took not only accurate information but also a number of errors—some of which he probably recognised as errors, and some of which must have deceived him as they would deceive most other readers of the directory. Furthermore, Joyce must have realised that *Thom's* contained mistakes which he would overlook, but which he might nonetheless, unwittingly, transcribe into *Ulysses*, possibly incorporating in the process of transcription, or permitting in subsequent processes like the typesetting and proofreading of his novel, the addition of still more errors. As Clive Hart and Leo Knuth observe, 'in cases like these, where Joyce is recreating not only the "real" Dublin but also the Dublin which was mediated through the daughters of memory and the printing presses, fact becomes inextricably intertwined with fiction' (Hart and Knuth 15). The relationship of *Ulysses* to the world outside it, moreover, assumed in the process degrees of ironic elaboration and intricacy sufficient to satisfy even Joyce, whose awareness of the potential complexity of the relationship between text and world surely exceeds that of any other novelist.

8
Conclusion

This chapter asks what happens when readers of *Ulysses* attempt to combine, in their cumulative and considered response to the novel, the text's various modes of irony, which have been successively evaluated earlier in this book. This investigation necessarily leads us to the question of Joyce's purposes in deploying such a variety of modes, the question of the effects which he intended his complex ironic texture to generate. Finally, and as an inevitable consequence, we must assess Joyce's few explicit declarations about the nature of irony and what it could do for him.

We need to remember that irony always assumes, and sometimes actually asserts, a duality of some kind. Overt meanings relate dualistically, and even symmetrically, to concealed meanings. Although we may occasionally reflect, when we encounter an instance of irony, that textual meanings are not unitary and may therefore be multiple, that a semantic uncertainty asserted by irony undermines such cosy structures as dualities, we must nevertheless devote our primary attention to the relationship between two semantic layers or locations.

Yet interconnections within texts, and between texts and external entities, often transgress or transcend dualistic structures. If we only consider individual instances of irony, however widely diverse in type, we remain confined to a theoretical and schematic assumption about structure which may fail to correspond to our practical reading experience. In *Ulysses* Joyce evokes delineations of experience and attitudes to life which function in countless dimensions. If irony operates in the novel as centrally and essentially as this study has argued, we need to link the dual structure of irony with the multiple structure of Joyce's text.

Such a linkage appears when we reflect on relationships among the divergent types of irony so far considered. These relationships may sometimes take specific, unique and uncharacteristic form: a particular local irony operating within a single episode, for example, might qualify a larger irony requiring in Joyce's readers some knowledge of the historical Dublin. If, however, a consistent direction or pattern appears among the various ironic modes, it may simultaneously free the author from the essentially dualistic nature of ironic operations, add new thematic emphases of its own, and considerably enrich the implications of the text.

The structure of the present book depends on the belief that Joyce's modes of irony can be analysed most clearly when classified by scale: it seems logical, in other words, to begin by assessing the more minute and local ironies and to move progressively outwards into a series of encounters with the larger and more wide-ranging examples. Although even the most local instances of irony may be difficult to resolve, they do require (by definition) only their immediate context within a particular episode to allow their adequate explication. The less specific, less local ironies demand increasingly elaborate comparisons and the invocation of a second component which becomes progressively more difficult to find.

This sequence of analysis also rests on, and expresses, certain assumptions about the structure of *Ulysses*. The novel appears here as spatial rather than temporal, as disjunctive more than consecutive. Even a reader who encounters the book only once, and reads it sequentially, may respond to these characteristics of the text. On subsequent readings, as further connections among textual components appear, the structure appears even more emphatically non-consecutive; indeed, the inadequacy of analytic modes which depend upon consecutive operations becomes at times a specific target of the novel's own rhetoric.

A reader who responds to the novel's broad range of ironies should experience an enhancement of the process of re-evaluation which the text necessarily demands from those who encounter it. Irony tends to prompt numerous and progressive re-evaluations of textual components and their relationships. In these terms, the reader will usually notice ironies in the sequence delineated here: the most specifically local ironies appear first, the most wide-ranging ones only after considerable experience of the text.

If, then, Joyce makes ironic use of the relationships among different ironic modes, he will almost inevitably prefer to have the more intricate types of irony work to qualify the more straightforward ones, since readers will usually detect the ironies in this sequence. Our expectation that a local irony, once recognised, constitutes a semantic totality closely resembles (if in a more intricate dimension) our initial assumptions about determined, single and non-ironic meanings. This expectation may, however, be subject to parallel strategies of ironic qualification. Irony, itself, thus remains accessible to ironic treatment.

Though an irony characteristic of one particular mode may sometimes receive qualification through another irony in the same mode, more emphatic semantic adjustments occur when another type is invoked instead. The use of a different, broader kind of irony to qualify a more specific one becomes Joyce's nearly invariable practice in *Ulysses*. He clearly anticipates the process by which a reader learns to respond to increasingly wide-ranging ironic operations; and he rewards the reader by ensuring that (with a few exceptions) all the instances of inter-modal ironic qualification work in the same direction.

The structure and sequence of the present study therefore assume, additionally, that cases of inter-modal irony in the text of *Ulysses* mostly operate in the direction delineated here.

If broader ironies do consistently qualify more local ones, certain consequences necessarily follow. The text tends to become outward-looking rather than involuted. An ironic, wholly internal cross-reference will frequently be revalued by a reference leading outside the novel. And the further it leads us from the immediate context in the novel, the more radically it may qualify the internal cross-reference. All these structural characteristics of *Ulysses* have thematic implications. They support concerns and emphases which the text also conveys through its deployment of plot and character. Thus 'outward-looking' attitudes and modes of behaviour progressively manifest their superiority to 'involuted' ones, a pattern embodied most obviously in the displacement of our attention from Stephen to Bloom and then to Molly. The novel suggests that an impulse to regard the world as a set of closed systems is a false, limiting and self-defeating view; each system, properly regarded, eludes closure and asserts affinities or analogies with components of other systems. At a more purely metaphysical level, fictive elements show themselves to be firmly grounded in a 'real' world existing prior to, and beyond, the text of the novel.

We need now to evaluate Joyce's own comments on the subject of irony.

Irony may inevitably be a difficult topic for its practitioners to discuss openly, since its successful operation depends on obliquity and indirection, on the transmission from author to reader of messages which are encoded rather than explicit. Though critics must theorise about irony and analyse particular instances, creative writers may find it unhelpful or even impossible to do so. While Joyce's works, especially *Ulysses*, exploit ironic modes with remarkable energy and variety, he usually refrains from conveying his own views on the subject of irony within those works themselves. One exceptionally direct (but still enigmatic) mention, already discussed in the first chapter of this book, occurs in his early essay 'A Portrait of the Artist'. His draft novel *Stephen Hero*, which among Joyce's writings is uncharacteristically explicit (and which, partly because of that very explicitness, was never brought by Joyce to the stage of publication), also includes a brief but revealing passage which we might apply, judiciously, to the author himself as well as to his character Stephen Daedalus:

> In his expressions of love he [Stephen] found himself
> compelled to use what he called the feudal terminology
> and as he could not use it with the same faith and
> purpose as animated the feudal poets themselves he was
> compelled to express his love a little ironically. This
> suggestion of relativity, he said, mingling itself with so
> immune a passion is a modern note: we cannot swear or
> expect eternal fealty because we recognise too accurately
> the limits of every human energy.   (*SH* 174)

Here, Joyce seems to acknowledge the value of irony in
assisting literary detachment, objectivity and relativism.
Later in his career, however, Joyce would suppress any such
overt pronouncements in his fiction.

Nor does he discuss the subject of irony expansively in any
of his surviving 'non-fictional' texts. Joyce's published literary criticism, for example, treats the topic of irony only
fleetingly or obliquely. In a review written in 1903 and largely
concerned with Giordano Bruno, he remarks that Bruno's
'excursions into that treacherous region from which even
ironical Aristotle did not come undiscredited, the science of
morality, have an interest only because they are so fantastical
and middle-aged' (*CW* 133). Here, Joyce implies that irony
may serve as a defensive strategy, necessary to cope with the
world's obduracy or complexity. But such comments remain
rare in his criticism.

Joyce's published letters show his reticence in dealing with
many literary topics and especially with the detailed mechanics of his own writing; irony is perhaps the most extreme
example of a literary practice which seems ubiquitous and
crucial in his creative works but remains essentially and
pointedly ignored in his own accounts of them. The letters,
then, show that if Joyce ever formulated a theory of irony, he
refrained from confiding the fact to his relatives, friends,
associates and publishers. Irony, we suspect, served the
same purpose as the 'puzzles' and 'enigmas' which he said he
had deployed in *Ulysses*, whose details he also avoided
discussing.

Part of his strategy in *Ulysses* involves the concealment of vital components beneath dissembling exteriors, both bland and strident. The novel was intended to release its meaning only slowly, as a community of readers painstakingly learnt how to respond to its revolutionary methods of communicating. This strategy required Joyce to suppress hints which he must have been tempted to supply to readers struggling with the intricacies of his text. That he did mostly suppress such information shows his confidence in the ability of his novel to explain itself, and his recognition that he had chosen literary methods which might be undermined if he provided explicit accounts of them. The most important such method is irony.

Joyce's closest approach to direct critical instruction came in his insistence that *Ulysses* was a complex work incorporating disparate and seemingly contradictory elements, none of which should be overlooked. As Ellmann says, 'to those who read the book as an ordinary work of fiction, [Joyce] wished to make clear its elaborate structure; to those who addressed themselves to the structure, he pointed to the novelistic element' (Ellmann 1977: 24). But of course such a sly mode of explication, while direct by Joyce's standards, also possesses its own ironic dimensions.

Even Joyce's famous 'schemata' for *Ulysses*, copies of which he sometimes entrusted to friends with the apparent intention of wider distribution, complicate our response to the novel as much as they elucidate it. The schemata usefully draw attention to such elements as the Homeric analogies, providing authorial support for valid and often illuminating interpretations which might otherwise be occasionally doubtful or even overlooked altogether. But the schemata contain their own traps, and might best be seen as a further layer of ironic suggestion surrounding the novel and protecting it from oversimplified readings. Cheryl Herr remarks in her essay 'Art and Life, Nature and Culture, *Ulysses*':

> The schemata cannot be considered authoritative guides to the fiction, for they are themselves only Joyce's

fictions about *Ulysses*. . . . Both from within and from without *Ulysses* announces its approximation to a nature that is in fact absent from the work. The stream-of-consciousness technique, which seems to transcribe real thoughts and their typical patterns of association, may be more accurately described as documenting the emergence of what appear to be personal thoughts from an impersonal environment of conventions and texts. The schemata, which have long been used as external but reasonably reliable abstracts of *Ulysses*, must be recognized as signifying a wholeness or encyclopedism that they in fact undermine from within as they present more lacunae and differentiations than clues to coherence.

(Newman and Thornton 29-30)

Joyce's letters, though they disclose little information about his attitudes to irony as a literary phenomenon, nevertheless serve obliquely to remind us of several further reasons why it commended itself to him. Apparently he intended some of the letters to convey such suggestions, since he lingers over biographical data which have clear analogies in his choice of literary methods like irony, analogies which he obviously expects his correspondents to notice. But the letters to various correspondents, read today in a posthumous collected edition and in a sequence which Joyce could not have anticipated, also convey such hints to us in a necessarily less premeditated manner.

Irony usually involves semantic disturbance, uncertainty, transference and relocation; the replacement of overt meanings by concealed ones; and the process of adjusting one's own value judgments or of prompting others to adjust their value judgments. All these phenomena interested Joyce in varying contexts, literary and otherwise: his development as a writer, his teaching of language and persistent assimilation of new languages, and his evolving and complex relationship to Ireland. In particular, Joyce's multi-lingual capabilities and contexts helped to refine his gift for expressing meanings in oblique, elaborate and multiple ways, and for recognising precisely which mode of direct or indirect communication would best serve his purposes in a particular situation. As Mason and Ellmann point out, during the years 1904-14 Joyce published virtually nothing in English; instead, 'he expressed himself directly and publicly only in the nine articles he wrote for the Triestine newspaper, *Il Piccolo della Sera*, and in the lectures he gave to a popular audience in Trieste. In them his irony has become more subdued and deliberate, still keen but more ingratiating' (*CW* 9).

Joyce's letters also show us his gift for adjusting his register when addressing different correspondents and dealing with various situations. All letter-writers make this kind of adjustment to some extent, but Joyce's registers diverge more radically than those of most people. As Gilbert remarks, 'there is no question that as a stylist Joyce was capable [in *Ulysses*] of chameleon-like changes and one would be hard put to it to decide which style was "naturally" Joyce's. We find much the same thing in the letters; the writer's skill in adjusting their tone, not merely their content, to the personality of his correspondents is quite remarkable' (*L I* 31). (Of course, Joyce adjusts the tone and content of his letters in response to other factors besides the 'personality' of his correspondent of the moment; his immediate rhetorical purposes often provide a more conspicuous reason for such adjustments.) It appears that Joyce enjoys the process of cultivating a persona particularly appropriate (or, in some cases, inappropriate) to a given correspondent or situation.

Perhaps, also, Joyce enjoys the diversity among these personae and his own ability to move easily from one to another. A further analogy with photographs of Joyce suggests itself; as Kenner has pointed out, in each case when Joyce poses for a picture he seems to adopt a particular and well-formulated role: 'We see Joyce playacting whenever a camera is trained on him: as Rimbaud, as Mephisto, as Blind Jim, as *père de famille*; one would hardly believe that many of his photographs are of the same man. And he *used* roles, of course, to keep people at a manipulable distance' (Hart and Hayman 342). Joyce may thus have practised, in his letter-writing and in other contexts which required him to assume a role or adopt a mask, skills of register choice, impersonation or ventriloquism which he also deployed in his fiction. Irony always involves a choice of register, and requires the ability to use a chosen register to convey particular implications; thus it seems likely that Joyce's preferred modes of correspondence tended further to encourage his literary use of irony.

Joyce's letters, furthermore, parallel his literary works in their deployment of particular geographical settings as an ironic mirror of the feelings of an observer. The letters which Joyce wrote from Dublin to Trieste during his return visits to Ireland in 1909-12, for example, stress his disillusioned and critical view of his native city. Much of his account of Dublin given in these letters, however, is really a description of his own feelings, projected onto a landscape which had helped him to develop and to understand those feelings. In his fiction, Joyce regularly uses urban environments and back-grounds with a similar awareness of their potential for ironic correlation or corroboration.

The circumstances of Joyce's life, perhaps especially those on which he meditated at length in his correspondence, must in themselves have fostered his conscious awareness of ironic possibilities. The family rootlessness and social decline which marked his childhood and adolescence in Dublin doubtless left him sceptical about fixed standing places and points of observation, and a similar scepticism (and social instability) also characterised his later years. It seems he increasingly suspected that apparent and real meanings were bound to diverge, that no statement made to him (by a publisher, for example) could be taken at face value. Joyce came to feel that other people often contrived, deliberately or otherwise, to increase the awkwardness and difficulty of his circumstances, and that his own attempts to ameliorate those circumstances would therefore remain condemned to a degree of futility. On 11 February 1907, for example, he wrote to Stanislaus

Joyce: '*Of course* just the very week I wanted it most Aunt J did not send *Sinn Féin*' (*L II* 211, italics added).

Thus an acceptance of the inescapable 'irony of circumstances' increasingly supplemented Joyce's sense of the ubiquity of irony as an aspect of semantic transactions. Ellmann delineates another ironic mode which appears in many of the letters: 'In retrospect, it is clear that Joyce's secret motive in making most of his threats . . . was to compel the contrapuntal encouragement which would warrant his not fulfilling them' (*L II* xxxvii). Ellmann comments further that the ironies Joyce deploys in his letters may 'be said to compete with each other. At one end of the scale he filters self-abasement through mockery; at the other, he approaches grandeur, feels it verging on grandiosity, and turns abruptly away' (*L II* xliii). And while literary critics should encroach onto psychological topics only with great caution, it is difficult to overlook the potential link between Joyce's highly ambivalent feelings about many subjects—Ireland is an obvious example—and an affinity for irony, with its capacity for indirection, ability to balance between competing implications, and alertness to contradiction.

Joyce's life, especially as depicted in his letters, seems to expand exponentially in complexity, to pile further complications atop existing ones. (Ellmann remarks that when Joyce had made his life intolerably intricate in one location he would not attempt to untangle the complexities, but preferred instead to move to a new setting where the process of complication might begin again.) This biographical process closely parallels the evolution of his literary texts from lyrical slightness in *Chamber Music* to encyclopedic complexity in *Finnegans Wake*; and his restless exploration, in successive works, of radically diverse genres—each work differing generically from everything which he had written previously and differing also, in the cases of *Ulysses* and especially *Finnegans Wake*, from everything which anyone else had written previously. The biographical pattern also parallels, more specifically, the structure of ironic revaluation which operates in *Ulysses*, where larger ironies qualify, and so reveal the limitations of, more restricted ones.

Joyce's habit of living in places whose first language was not English, besides accentuating his tendency to approach the English language as if from outside (a tendency which has been fruitfully analysed by several recent critics), must have encouraged his experiments with irony. Detachment from his native linguistic context and immersion in 'foreign' language milieux, paralleling his geographical and political position, must have enhanced his sense of the possible ironic disjunctions which may separate various ways of expressing a given meaning. Awareness and exploration of irony seem inevitable aspects of Joyce's life, given his particular conjunction of experiences: teaching English in distant and 'foreign' parts of Europe, reflecting on his complex relationships with Dublin and Ireland, and writing experimental works of literature.

Irony, as a literary method, also seems entirely compatible with the manifesto of 'silence, exile, and cunning' which Stephen Dedalus expresses in the *Portrait* (*P* 247) and which closely parallels Joyce's own youthful credo. Irony exhibits and evokes 'cunning', since it requires considerable wiliness from both writer and reader; it elicits particular skills which equip a reader to deal with it, and so calls into being an audience able to respond to the author's (potentially subversive) statements. It aligns itself readily with 'exile', partly in ways already discussed above, but also by enhancing the awareness of detachment and divergent perspectives which social and geographical isolation tends to impart; and it reinforces the notion that exile is a spiritual state shared by those who become capable of such detached insight, a kind of exile which Joyce treats quite explicitly in his play *Exiles*. And irony consorts even with 'silence', since it involves the suppression of overt meanings and a reliance on the knowing reader to reconstruct implications which have been imparted only obliquely. By 'silence', Stephen and Joyce never did intend the complete extinction of self-expression, but rather an insistence on saying only what they wished to say in the way they wished to say it, and an escape from conventional declarations and confessions about their chosen manner of life. Irony lends itself to those types of self-expression which Stephen and Joyce, having proclaimed their allegiance to silence, felt they might still allow themselves.

If irony operates as pervasively and variously in *Ulysses* as this study has argued, one of the novel's most central themes must necessarily be a demonstration of—even an insistence on—the ironical nature of the world Joyce depicts. Yet if irony accords with numerous positive implications, as this study has also claimed, that conclusion need not seem regrettable or even problematic. Booth has commented negatively on literary texts which seem to be written for the sake of the irony. But such an undertaking may have positive value. Esteemed literary works have been written to show that experience is (or can be) tragic or comic; they may surely be written with equal logic to show that experience is or can be ironic. They may, in other words, seek to illustrate that the world needs to be approached obliquely, that meanings may be deceptive and require constant revaluation, and that apparently self-contradictory qualities often require considerable relativistic flexibility to understand. This view of life would be widely (and perhaps increasingly) endorsed by modern observers. It is one of the many achievements of *Ulysses* that it demonstrates so comprehensively, as much by structural as by thematic means, how plausible and necessary such a view of the world may be.

Bibliography

Adams, Robert Martin, *Surface and Symbol: The Consistency of James Joyce's Ulysses*, New York: Oxford Univ. Press, 1962.

Booth, Wayne C., *A Rhetoric of Irony*, Chicago: Univ. of Chicago Press, 1974.

Bushrui, Suheil Badi, and Bernard Benstock, edd., *James Joyce: An International Perspective*, Gerrards Cross, Bucks: Colin Smythe, 1982.

Butler, Samuel, *The Authoress of the Odyssey*, London: Jonathan Cape, 1922.

Butler, Samuel *Collected Essays*, 1925, New York: AMS Press, 1968.

Card, James Van Dyck, *An Anatomy of 'Penelope'*, Cranbury, N. J.: Associated University Presses, 1984.

Cixous, Hélène, *The Exile of James Joyce*, transl. Sally A. J. Purcell, New York: David Lewis, 1972.

Ellmann, Richard, *The Consciousness of Joyce*, Toronto: Oxford Univ. Press, 1977.

Ellmann, Richard, *James Joyce*, rev. edn New York: Oxford Univ. Press, 1982.

Ellmann, Richard, *Ulysses on the Liffey*, London: Faber & Faber, 1972.

Enright, D. J., *The Alluring Problem: An Essay on Irony*, Oxford: Oxford Univ. Press, 1986.

Epstein, Edmund L., *The Ordeal of Stephen Dedalus: The Conflict of the Generations in James Joyce's A Portrait of the Artist as a Young Man*, Carbondale: Southern Illinois Univ. Press, 1971.

French, Marilyn, *The Book as World: James Joyce's Ulysses*, Cambridge, Mass: Harvard Univ. Press, 1976.

Gilbert, Stuart, *James Joyce's Ulysses: A Study*, rev. edn London: Faber & Faber, 1952.

Goldberg, S. L., *The Classical Temper: A Study of James Joyce's Ulysses*, London: Chatto & Windus, 1961.

Gordon, John, *James Joyce's Metamorphoses*, Dublin: Gill & Macmillan, 1981.

Gose, Elliott B., *The Transformation Process in Joyce's Ulysses*, Toronto: Univ. of Toronto Press, 1980.

Gottfried, Roy, 'Reading Figather: Tricks of the Eye in *Ulysses*', *James Joyce Quarterly*, 25 (1988), 465-74.

Hart, Clive, and David Hayman, edd., *James Joyce's Ulysses: Critical Essays*, Berkeley: Univ. of California Press, 1974.

Hart, Clive, and Leo Knuth, *A Topographical Guide to James Joyce's Ulysses*, Colchester: A Wake Newslitter Press, 1975.

Hayman, David, *Ulysses: The Mechanics of Meaning*, rev. edn Madison, Wisconsin: Univ. of Wisconsin Press, 1982.

Henke, Suzette A., *Joyce's Moraculous Sindbook: A Study of Ulysses*, Columbus, Ohio: Ohio State Univ. Press, 1978.

Herring, Phillip F., 'The Bedsteadfastness of Molly Bloom', *Modern Fiction Studies*, 15 (1969), 49-61.

Herring, Phillip F., *Joyce's Uncertainty Principle*, Princeton: Princeton Univ. Press, 1987.

Homer, *The Odyssey*, transl. S. H. Butcher and A. Lang, London: Macmillan, 1887.

Homer, *The Odyssey*, transl. E. V. Rieu, Harmondsworth: Penguin, 1946.

Kain, Richard M., 'The Significance of Stephen's Meeting Bloom: A Survey of Interpretations', *James Joyce Quarterly*, 10 (1972), 147-60.

Kenner, Hugh, *A Colder Eye: The Modern Irish Writers*, New York: Knopf, 1983.

Kenner, Hugh, *Dublin's Joyce*, London: Chatto & Windus, 1956.

Kenner, Hugh, *Joyce's Voices*, Berkeley: Univ. of California Press, 1978.

Kenner, Hugh, *Ulysses*, London: Allen & Unwin, 1980.

Kimball, Jean, 'The Measure of Bloom—Again', *James Joyce Quarterly*, 18 (1981), 201-4.

Lang, Candace D., *Irony/Humor: Critical Paradigms*, Baltimore: Johns Hopkins Univ. Press, 1988.

Lawrence, Karen, *The Odyssey of Style in Ulysses*, Princeton: Princeton Univ. Press, 1981.

MacCabe, Colin, *James Joyce and the Revolution of the Word*, London: Macmillan, 1978.

Mahaffey, Vicki, *Reauthorizing Joyce*, Cambridge: Cambridge Univ. Press, 1988.

Melchiori, Giorgio, 'The Rev. John Flynn and Buck Mulligan', *James Joyce Quarterly*, 27 (1989), 124-6.

Muecke, D. C., *Irony and the Ironic*, rev. edn London: Methuen, 1982.

Murillo, L. A., *The Cyclical Night: Irony in James Joyce and Jorge Luis Borges*, Cambridge, Mass.: Harvard Univ. Press, 1968.

Newman, Robert D., and Weldon Thornton, edd., *Joyce's Ulysses: The Larger Perspective*, Cranbury, N. J.: Associated University Presses, 1987.

Sandulescu, C. George, and Clive Hart, edd., *Assessing the 1984 Ulysses*, Gerrards Cross, Bucks.: Colin Smythe, 1986.

Schutte, William M., *Joyce and Shakespeare: A Study in the Meaning of Ulysses*, New Haven: Yale Univ. Press, 1957.

Schwarz, Daniel R., *Reading Joyce's Ulysses*, New York: St. Martin's Press, 1987.

Scott, Bonnie Kime, *James Joyce*, Brighton: Harvester Press, 1987.

Seidel, Michael, *Epic Geography: James Joyce's Ulysses*, Princeton: Princeton Univ. Press, 1976.

Senn, Fritz, *Joyce's Dislocutions: Essays on Reading as Translation*, ed. John Paul Riquelme, Baltimore: Johns Hopkins Univ. Press, 1984.

Shakespeare, William, *Hamlet*, ed. John Dover Wilson, Cambridge: Cambridge Univ. Press, 1969.

States, Bert O., *Irony and Drama: A Poetics*, Ithaca: Cornell Univ. Press, 1971.

Van Caspel, Paul, *Bloomers on the Liffey: Eisegetical Readings of Joyce's Ulysses*, Baltimore: Johns Hopkins Univ. Press, 1986.

Index

Where entries give many page references, the main passages are indicated in italic type.